MINDFUL EATING FOR LASTING WEIGHT LOSS

SURROUND YOURSELF WITH MINDFUL MOMENTS FOR LONG-TERM WEIGHT LOSS

SIMONE E. CLARK

CONTENTS

AS A GIFT TO YOU!

THE MINDFUL MOMENTS CHECKLIST -
(START YOUR MINDFUL MOMENTS
TODAY!!!)

MINDFUL MOMENTS CHECKLIST

THIS CHECKLIST INCLUDES:

- 8 suggested methods of mindful moments to take in a month
- Spaces for you to fill out your mindful moment, a week at a time

- Reuse this mindful moment checklist over and over again
- 7 resources to help find those mindful moments and where you can find these resources

To receive your free mindful moments checklist and bullet points, visit this link:

https://simoneeclark.activehosted.com/f/1

Be sure to check out my Facebook group - https://rb.gy/bfpcf5

INTRODUCTION

Our bodies are always reaching out and longing for nutrients and assistance, and we are the only ones who can provide this essential need. Just look at how your body reacts when you have too much alcohol or too much sugar or too little fiber. Everything in your life has an impact on your health, be it your family or your emotions or stress. If you don't treat your body with love and care, it might not return the favor. The problem is that most people have difficulty finding a balanced relationship with food, resulting in their inability to lose weight or keep it off. This is a challenge because people tend to only look at the scale instead of looking at their relationship with food. They are unsure about the methods that would help them create honest, reflective moments that would give their bodies time to figure out whether they want a particular food or not. If you're one of these people, then you're in the right place. In this book, I'm going to address these issues and guide you on how to develop mindful moments that can help bring in intuitive eating.

There are moments in every person's life where they must choose their health above everything else, which might not be easy. You cannot achieve that in one day. It will take time, and you have to be patient, but with the right steps in the right direction, you will make it to a point where you can intentionally go into a moment knowing you have the power to choose what is right for you. This is where you are going to learn the art of mindful eating. In recent times, you have most likely heard others talking about mindful eating and how it can help you reduce weight and keep it off. Once you start reading this book, you realize that mindful eating is not a very complicated concept to grasp. Unfortunately, most people back out just because they are overwhelmed; and do not have access to the right information.

In this book, I am going to help you understand the definition of mindful eating. I will help you understand the concepts of mind-body connections, and slowly but steadily, you will learn how to differentiate between what you need and what you merely want. Through the techniques of mindful eating, you will be able to bring awareness to everything that is happening inside your body, your mind, as well as in the world around you. Honoring this kind of knowledge can help you understand how various foods affect your body, mind, and day-to-day experiences.

My name is Simone Clark, and I have been helping people as a health coach for years. I have helped them structure their goals properly and showed them how they could achieve those goals through a realistic approach. With my help, they have been able to see things in a new light, and by implementing mindfulness strategies, they now have a much healthier relationship with food. This book is a result of my passion for this field and my love of all things related to wellness. I want to help people who have been struggling with weight loss. Through this book, I am going to help you implement intuitive and mindful strategies so you can come to a place of peace in your mind, have the aftereffect of weight loss, and, in turn, not gain this weight back.

After you understand how mindfulness can change your whole world around, your daily actions and belief systems are going to undergo a radical change. You will no longer be fretting over what you ate or didn't eat because the word 'diet' is no longer going to control your life. Your daily actions will become the lifestyle changes that will help you distinguish between whether or not you want to eat a particular food. You will finally be able to escape the toxic habit of labeling food as good or bad. Instead, you will learn to ask yourself whether you love the food you are eating or not. You will learn to understand how your body reacts to different food items. Over time, mindful eating will encourage you to create space for healthy food choices, and weight loss and other health benefits will come naturally as a result.

The way my clients keep thanking me for all that they have attained in life is proof of my experience and how much I can help you to change your mindset and outlook. I am going to address these issues head-on. There is no need to make things complicated when you can come to the table with peace and rest in your mind.

So, are you ready to take on your journey towards better health? With my help and expertise, you will have advanced knowledge of every hurdle that might come your way on this journey. With the help of this book, forming a daily habit can become so much easier. You can learn to bring in mindful moments with the skills and knowledge given in this book. You can also learn to implement intuitive eating habits that will help you lose weight and maintain that loss. Even in unfortunate situations, like an unexpected tragedy or a disease, following the techniques mentioned in the book, you will be able to make healthier choices for the long-term and indulge in mindful moments.

The book you are about to read will offer you tangible ways

to implement mindful eating to help change the way you think and urge you to adopt a mindful way of living. You are thereby making healthier choices that could help in weight loss. Every chapter will provide you with actionable steps that will help you reach your goals. If you follow the methods mentioned in this book, you will soon be on your way to mindset changes, thought pattern turnarounds, and weight loss that stays off for good.

1

WHAT IS MINDFUL EATING AND WHAT DOES IT MEAN FOR YOU?

E very year, thousands of people embark on the same journey to get healthy and lose weight. Not only do we want to live more energetically, but we also want to feel better about ourselves. However, there is one major roadblock at the core of all these changes: our profoundly ingrained eating habits. Even though we know that we should change our practices, we often fail to understand how to do that. Several conventional diets can offer quick and straight forward solutions. However, these diets tend to do more harm than good and might hurt both your health and self-esteem.

Have you come across the phrase 'mindful eating'? It is a method by which you can gain control over your eating habits. Mindful eating involves paying attention to how you are eating and being aware so that you eat just enough to feel satisfied.

WHAT IS MINDFUL EATING?

Mindful eating is a technique based on the Buddhist Zen concept of mindfulness (Nelson, 2017). Mindfulness is a kind of meditation that can help you understand and cope with your physical sensations and emotions. Mindful eating makes use of mindfulness to reach a state of full attention and assists in helping you understand your cravings and physical cues while eating. It is not a modern-day concept. The approach of mindful eating has been tried by many, tested, refined, and used by a vast number of people in every kind of diet and culture, for many, many years.

Jon Kabat-Zinn defined the term mindfulness as a particular way of paying attention to things purposefully and non-judgmentally in the present moment. He was the original leader and developer of the Mindfulness-Based Stress Reduction program conducted at the University of Mass-achusetts Medical School. Moreover, in the year 1990, he wrote a book called 'Full Catastrophe Living' based on his experiences with the program since the year 1979 so that he could guide others on how to live mindfully.

The meaning of the term mindfulness is more significant

than how we use it in our everyday language. It urges one to be aware of whatever the focus might be and thus has gained a lot of popularity. It has become a way of encouraging someone to take good care of her or himself. Similarly, we can be encouraged to gain awareness of our eating experiences through mindful eating.

The practice of mindfulness has encouraged many people to live more intentionally and acquire the necessary skills to manage anxiety, depression, diseases, chronic pain, and sleeping problems. It has also emerged as the focus of an approach to eating that satisfies the criteria that are essential for changing one's eating habits. The fact that diet is useless without behavioral changes has been recognized for quite some time now. Diets might be useful in the short term; they might also be ineffective in the long run.

The approach of mindful eating focuses on our sensual awareness of the food we are eating and our experience while eating it. It has little to do with the amount of protein, fat, carbohydrates, or the overall calories present in what we are eating. The main focus of mindful eating is not weight loss. However, people who follow this lifestyle are more likely to lose weight. The purpose of mindful eating is to encourage your full presence while you are eating and help you savor the food and the moments.

Mindful eating involves the following attitudes:

- **Beginner's mindset** – Approaching your experiences from the mentality of a baby enables you to experience them anew. Try to engage your senses by noticing the flavor, texture, sounds, smells, and colors of the foods.

- **Patience** – You need to be patient to eat mindfully. Take your time to be aware of each moment. Eat slowly and without any distraction to experience the full process rather than racing through it.

- **Non-judgment** – Being aware of our judgment is one of the essential elements of mindful eating. Our first challenge is to begin consuming the food by setting aside our experience of the food.

- **Acceptance** – Acceptance is the core of the process of mindful eating. We should develop a willingness to accept whatever happens at the moment as it is.

- **Trust** – We develop more self-trust by gaining full awareness of our own experiences and by accepting them. This is our experience, and it might be different from anyone else's experience. We end up becoming more accepting of ourselves by noticing and appreciating what we see, feel, and our personal experience of the different foods.

- **Non-striving** – While diets tend to be all about

striving for weight loss, mindful eating is in clear contrast to it. As a consumer, I am allowed to fully appreciate the experience by being in the moment as no specific outcomes are being measured. There is no particular outcome that can be expected through mindful eating.

- **Letting go** – Letting go of our past resentments and other expectations about foods are essential for mindful eating moments. Letting go will allow us to fully experience new things in the here and now, without harboring any past judgments.

These attitudes are imperative in the foundation of mindful eating. They are interconnected and similar to each other, which allows them to work well together.

WHY SHOULD YOU TRY MINDFUL EATING?

In today's fast-paced society, we always get tempted by the boundless choices of food. Other distractions like smartphones, computers, and televisions also tend to shift our attention away from the act of eating. Therefore, eating has turned into a mindless action, which we often do too fast. As our brain takes up to twenty minutes to understand when we're full, it can become a problem.

When we eat too quickly, the fullness signal might arrive

after we have already eaten beyond our capacity. This is commonly seen in binge eating.

By following the technique of mindful eating, we can make eating an intentional act rather than an automatic one by slowing down and restoring our attention. Moreover, by trying to understand the cues of fullness and physical hunger, we can differentiate between real physical hunger and emotional hunger. We can also enhance our understanding of the triggers that make us want to eat, although we are not hungry. We can create a space between our triggers and our responses when we become aware of our triggers. This awareness could help us by providing us with the time and freedom to choose how we want to react.

HOW TO PRACTICE MINDFUL EATING?

There are many simple ways to practice mindful eating. You can begin by quietly sitting in a comfortable position, fully alert with your eyes open. Then, monitor your hunger on a scale of one to seven, with one being very hungry and seven being uncomfortably full. Take a moment to understand how hungry you are at that moment. Try to differentiate between physical hunger and emotional hunger. We will discuss this topic in more detail in the latter part of this book. But for now, it's good to understand that while physical hunger starts gradually and can be postponed, emotional hunger can suddenly come and feels urgent. With physical hunger, you can stop eating once you are full. However, emotional hunger makes you feel uncomfortably full by making you eat more than you usually would.

When you are physically hungry, you can be satisfied with any kind of food. However, emotional hunger causes specific cravings and can leave you feeling guilty. Therefore, it can be wise to understand whether you are choosing to eat because of emotional hunger or physical hunger.

After understanding why you are hungry, take a deep breath to eliminate the air from your lungs. Let go of the tension present in your body by taking about three more intentional deep breaths.

Now, focus on the food placed in front of you and start the journey of mindful eating with each of your five senses.

- **See** – Look closely at the food you choose. How does your food look? Observe the color and shape of the food. Also, notice the area it takes up.
- **Smell** – Hold the food close to your nose and smell it. Try to understand how the smell makes you feel about eating the food.
- **Feel** – Gently pick up the food you choose and touch the surface. How does it feel? Does it feel soft, hard, round or oval, sticky, smooth, or prickly?

Knowing how it feels will help you in the process of mindful eating.

- **Taste** – Chew the food slowly and concentrate on the flavor, texture, and all the other sensations that you feel. Pay attention to whether the food is salty, sweet, bitter, or sour. Concentrate on your mouth salivating. Swallow the food only after experiencing it fully and observe how it moves down your esophagus as it moves into your stomach.

- **Hear** – Pay attention to any noises that might occur as the food runs through your body. Stop for some time, and then take another bite slowly. Concentrate on the sound of your teeth biting into the food.

Does your food feel satisfying? Did you enjoy its taste? Investigate your fullness and hunger by stopping and taking a breath between bites. Concentrate on how your stomach feels and whether you need another piece. Try to understand what your body is telling you. The process of eating mindfully might feel a little uncomfortable and awkward in the beginning. However, it will become more comfortable if you keep practicing day after day. Developing a realistic technique that works for you might take some time, but it will be worth it. So, the next time you eat something, pause and reflect on why you decided to eat that particular food before you take another bite.

Having a commitment to practice regularly and intentionally is also an essential aspect of following mindfulness. Practicing mindfulness regularly involves following a routine, which consists of planned and consistent mindful activities. Some of these activities are as follows:

- Develop self-awareness in your routine by noticing your breathing a few times during the day.
- Take part in a Yoga practice.
- Practice mindfulness meditation daily. It is a kind of sitting meditation that makes use of moment-to-moment awareness.
- Practice body scan meditations. Try tuning into your bodily sensations while you are meditating.
- Practicing mindful eating many times a week.
- Mindful walking every day.

These practices help us concentrate on each moment without any judgment, thereby developing a mindful approach towards living. Again, this may feel a bit overwhelming to think about implementing all of the steps above. Instead, try thinking about one or two of these to try out.

Mindful eating is all about helping you become aware of each bite or plate of food. It starts with the first thought of food and ends after the last bite is taken, and you experience the moment's result. The following are some suggestions that can be useful in teaching methods of mindful eating:

- Before automatically reaching for some food, pause for a short time, and try to understand what you are feeling at that moment and what you want to eat. Are you sad, angry, bored, lonely, or stressed? Or, are you physically hungry? Try to understand your reactivity and make the right choice for you.

- If you think that desire is not related to hunger, try doing something that is more appropriate to fulfill that desire.

- Put away any distractions (like your phone, TV, etc.) while you are eating and come to the table with intention and mindfulness. This action will help you pay attention to your food.

- Consider what it took to bring your food to you in addition to experiencing it. Think about the people who were involved in the process of growing and production. Take a moment to consider who made your food, where it comes from, and how it got to your table. Consider the sun and the soil where the ingredients were grown. Appreciate everything that happened in the process of getting food from the ground to your plate.

- Chew thoroughly.
- Savor every bite.
- Check-in with your body after every bite to understand how you are feeling. Consider whether you need more food or whether you've had enough. After that, you can move on to whatever you have decided. Stop eating when you feel full.

Practicing mindful eating also requires a commitment to bring changes in behavior similar to that required for any eating plan or diet. You can start by choosing one meal per day and focusing on these points. Mindfulness will become more natural when you get accustomed to it. After that, you can start implementing these habits into more meals.

The approach of mindful eating is not a quick fix; however, the benefits of including mindfulness are potentially life-altering. It allows us to focus on our freedom of choice, self-compassion, and awareness by letting go of the restrictions surrounding food.

TIPS FOR PRACTICING MINDFUL EATING

Here are some tips that you can follow while practicing mindful eating:

- **Stock foods that you like** – Eating mindfully doesn't involve eliminating certain foods from your diet or clearing out your cupboards. It comprises of being present in the moment, irrespective of what you are eating. So go ahead and fill up your cupboard with foods that you like eating. Then, sit down and be present while you enjoy every moment of eating your favorite food.

- **Try using a different utensil, or eat with your non-dominant hand** – To experience your food in a different way, try to mix things up. Are you left-handed? Try using your right hand, and vice versa. If you usually eat with the help of a fork, try eating with chopsticks. If you typically eat using chopsticks, try using a fork. Breaking our daily routines helps us think about our meals more deliberately, which can be fun as well.

- **Explore new flavors, textures, and tastes** – Try something new when you are cooking or eating out. Choose an ingredient, dish, or recipe that you've never had before. Eating mindfully is an excellent way to broaden your palate, embrace curiosity, and learn new things about your likes and dislikes.

Call to Action:

There will be a call to action after each chapter. Take a week at a time to work through these actions. You may finish each chapter within a week, but be sure to work through these steps for a full week before moving onto the next action. Take one meal for each of the next seven days. Use all your five senses to hone in on mindful eating. After listening to your hunger cues, take three deep breaths. Look at your meal and use all five senses to guide yourself through a mindful journey with that meal with no other distractions.

1. Take in a deep breath. What feelings does your meal bring up? What do you smell?
2. Look at your meal. What colors do you see?
3. Touch your meal with your hand or fork/spoon. Do you feel something hard or soft?
4. What do you hear around you? Is it your food steaming or cracking? Or do you just hear birds and conversations?
5. Take a bite. Does it taste sweet, salty, or bitter?

THE JOY OF EATING MINDFULLY

Mindful eating brings awareness to the meal, irrespective of what we chose to eat. It encourages a more holistic approach by bringing our focus to the how and why of eating. With this kind of awareness, mindful eating helps us rediscover our confidence and freedom. It also makes us watchful of what we eat. Therefore, we have an improved chance of knowing which foods help us stay healthy and nourish us. While also encouraging a deeper appreciation of all the ingredients, every mouthful, and every meal.

However, the benefits of mindful eating are subjective. Something healthy for one person might be unhealthy for another person. Therefore, it's clear that healthy cannot be defined by body shape or weight. Some of the benefits of eating mindfully are given below.

ENGAGES ALL FIVE SENSES

When was the last time you truly savored your meal experience and paid attention to what you were eating? We often consume our food on autopilot, chowing down on it while our mind is on a book, or the screen of our devices, or the TV or a daydream. Following the techniques of mindful eating, we can remove these distractions so that we can sit with our fellow diners and our food uninterrupted. By removing our distractions, we begin to take our time with our meal. We can savor the textures, the aromas, and the flavors by eating our food slowly. Mindful eating, thus, helps us reconnect with our senses.

We stop getting lost in our thoughts once we give our undivided attention to the full experience of eating. It also prevents us from getting caught up in any complicated emotions that might accompany a particular food. Simply put, through mindful eating, we allow ourselves to get re-accustomed with the pleasures of eating.

NO MORE RESTRICTIONS

Mindful eating, on its own, is not a diet. It doesn't include any quick fixes, any fads, or any radical cleanses. It doesn't require you to clear out your cupboards or eliminating certain foods. It is just a framework that aims to guide more mindful food choices, which might lead to a loss in weight.

However, it's worth noting that whenever we choose a food based on a particular result, we are not practicing mindful eating. We are consuming that food with a means to an end, and that can turn out to be potentially self-defeating. Mindful eating allows us to truly savor our food without any sense of personal commentary, anxiety, guilt, or judgment – by simply inviting us to be present when we are cooking or eating. This technique involves spending less time focusing on your weight and other weight-related issues. By embracing mindful eating, we can learn how to find the weight that is best suited for us naturally.

Conventional diet cultures tend to cause most of our stress around eating, usher in false expectations, and bring lots of pressure and intensity. As a result, most of us tend to see food as a punishment or a reward. It makes us think that we 'deserve' a specific spoonful or snack or bite of something and believe that it's our 'treat' as if we were a well-mannered child or dog. People who are overweight might ignore their feelings of fullness, whereas people who are obsessed with being thin might suppress their feelings of hunger and end up under-eating. Moreover, when people start internalizing the ideas around dieting and start believing the advertisements that suggest that weight loss is so effortless, then the emotions and pressures surrounding it get heightened. Mindful eating aims to undo these ideas and encourages us to let go of such traditional all-or-nothing thinking. It helps us to eat as per our natural bodyweight and not the bodyweight that is prescribed by media-fueled pressure and images portrayed in magazines. It does not include any strategy or counting of calories. It merely tries to make us aware.

Our mind gets calmer when we gain awareness. When our mind is quiet, we are less prone to getting stressed, agitated, or eat from an emotional place. Mindful eating also improves our clarity so we can notice our eating patterns more clearly. That clarity allows us to make better choices. We feel happier with the way we eat as we feel calmer and clearer. As we feel more content, clear, and calm, we feel more compassionate towards ourselves, making us less judgmental. The focus of mindful eating is not necessarily on changing the food we eat but changing our thinking around that food.

LISTENING TO THE GUT

Being aware of our emotions and thoughts, and being aware of everything that is occurring inside our stomach, adds another layer to our awareness.

As our blood sugar levels decrease when all the food present in our stomach gets burned, a hormone known as ghrelin gets released by our stomach. A signal is sent to the 'hunger center' present in our brains by the hormone ghrelin. The signal stimulates our appetite. Another hormone called leptin is secreted by the fat tissues when we are full. This hormone sends a signal to the brain when we are full. However, most scientists suggest that it takes about twenty minutes for our brains to receive the message. Thus, most of our overeating takes place during this period of twenty minutes.

By following the techniques of mindful eating, we can become more aware of the sensations that occur in our body before our brain registers satiety (the feeling of being satisfied). Mindful eating helps us tune in to our bodies so that we can better gauge when we feel full without having to wait for twenty minutes. Therefore, it helps us learn to be a step ahead of ourselves.

UNDERSTANDING WHAT OUR BODY NEEDS

Mindfulness refers to being present and interested and inquisitive about the food that's on our plate. It should also be accompanied by a willingness to explore the way we think and feel about things without any judgment.

Most people don't ask themselves questions like: How hungry am I? How full do I feel halfway through this meal? What does my body want? Am I enjoying my food or just scarfing it down? Am I not eating a particular food because I think it's 'bad' for me? Is this portion not enough for me, or is it too much?

A study (Monica Beshara, 2013) was conducted in 2013 to test the association between everyday mindfulness of people and the self-reported serving size of food. The serving size is considered a modifiable determinant of the consumption of energy and is an essential factor for the prevention and treatment of obesity. The study also explored the mediating role of eating mindfully. Self-report measures of mindful eating and everyday mindfulness of a community sample of 171 adults were reviewed. The participating adults who reported greater levels of everyday mindfulness had smaller serving size estimates of foods and were more mindful eaters. Eating mindfully mediated the negative connection between serving size and everyday mindfulness. The domains of mindful eating that are related to serving size are disinhibited and emotional eating. Thus, the results showed that people who followed the techniques of mindful eating properly ate smaller portions. This could help those people who are trying to lose weight, maintain a nutritional balance, or follow a fitness regime. However, this does not mean that eating mindfully requires you to eat small portions. You should consume whatever meal size is right for you.

Another thing that we can bring to the kitchen and super-market through mindful eating is awareness. It helps us to make choices based on our own internal knowledge of what is required by our bodies, rather than alternatives that are automatically influenced by impulses, emotions, or external thoughts. When our mind is left untrained, it can become susceptible to habit as well as emotional triggers. Our mind is a powerful thing, and it can be trained by meditation. Meditation helps us find the space that we require to make better choices that concern our overall weight and not our weight or body shape. The first question you should ask yourself to change this perspective is: What is your relation-ship to food?

UNDERSTANDING WHY WE EAT THE WAY WE EAT

Everyone's bodies are different, and in the same way, everyone has a different relationship to food. No one has a perfect body, and in the same way, there isn't a single ideal way to eat. Each of us has our priorities, preferences, metab-olisms, and genetics. While some of us graze, some gorge. Some comfort eat while some snack. Some overeat while others under eat. Some are obsessed with diets, always thinking about losing the pounds while some are gym freaks obsessed about increasing the pounds. Understanding who we are and being true to ourselves can help us understand why we eat the way we eat.

It requires a hand to reach out and pick a particular food. Food doesn't just jump from the shelves onto the plates. More often than not, the action of reaching out and choosing food is based on our emotions and thoughts associated with that food. We do this instead of a regime or considering a food's nutritional requirements or what's right for our bodies. By understanding how our feelings and beliefs influence our daily food intake and how we have been conditioned over the years, we can realize our eating patterns. When we learn to recognize those early influences, we can decide what to eat and when to eat it. What we choose to eat is our business alone; however, eating mindfully helps us understand what's right for our health and, subsequently, our bodies.

The effect of this awareness on people who overeat may be that they eat less, and for those who under eat, they may consume more. Others might notice that their eating patterns remain the same, but their thinking around food might change. Thus, mindful eating acts as an equalizer, which helps us find a balance in the way we relate to food.

BRINGS AWARENESS TO THE TABLE

Each of us has our attitudes or patterns of behavior associated with food, whether this is due to family situations, or genetics. Being aware of those origins helps us build the foundation of mindful eating. Mindfulness inserts a pause, which helps us become aware of our decision-making. It's similar to slowing down a recording and watching our process step by step: the cues, the feelings that kick in, and the full sensory impact of consuming food. We can begin changing our thinking or behavior about food only after we stop and notice this chain of events. With this observational awareness, we can notice how impulsive or reactive we appear at times. You can hone this skill by utilizing mindfulness. We are less inclined to feel any shame or guilt if we plan our restaurant menu, grocery list, or kitchen in advance.

Food is just – food. We can be better equipped to disregard any preconceived notions about food once we are able to acknowledge our dynamics around food and trace back our feelings about food. When we observe our minds in this way, we can remove any emotions that fuel our unhealthy habits. We don't need to eat our feelings, and in case we do, mindfulness helps us learn that we don't need to feel guilty about it.

Imagine how it would feel to no longer be led by our inner dialogue about food. Instead, imagine having a carefree and balanced attitude that is free from the shackles of unhealthy eating habits. Mindful eating helps us step away from all the negative and harmful feelings about food so that we can cultivate a balanced and sustainable approach towards the way we look and eat our food. It, therefore, helps us re-educate ourselves and enjoy our food again.

MINDFUL EATING AND BINGE EATING

Consuming a large quantity of food within a short period of time mindlessly and without intention, and any control is called binge eating. It has been linked to weight gain and various eating disorders. A study (Richard A. Grucza, 2007) revealed that about seventy percent of people who suffer from binge eating disorder suffer from obesity.

Eating mindfully can decrease the frequency and severity of binge eating episodes drastically. A literature review was conducted to determine the efficacy of mindfulness-based interventions (MBIs) for treating external eating, emotional eating, binge eating, and other obesity-related eating behaviors. Online databases were used to conduct a search protocol. A total of twenty-one papers were reviewed in this study. A variety of approaches were used to implement mindfulness training in these interventions. They included a combination of mindful exercises, mindful eating programs, acceptance-based therapies, mindfulness-based stress reduction, and combined mindfulness and cognitive behavioral therapy. Dietary intake, external eating, emotional eating, and binge eating were targeted behavior outcomes. Eighteen of the studies that were reviewed showed improvement in targeted eating behaviors. Thus, the results of the study (G. A. O'Reilly, 2014) support the effectiveness of MBIs for changing external eating, emotional eating, binge eating, and other obesity-related eating disorders.

Another study (Jean L. Kristeller, 1999) showed that after a six-week intervention in obese women, the binge eating episodes reduced from four to one and a half per week. There was a reduction in the severity of each episode as well.

MINDFUL EATING AND UNHEALTHY EATING BEHAVIORS

Apart from being effective in treating binge eating disorder, the techniques of mindful eating have also been shown to reduce:

- **External eating** – This takes place when we eat in response to cues related to the environment or food, like at the smell or sight of food.

- **Emotional eating** – When we eat in response to certain emotions, it is known as emotional eating.

People with obesity mostly report these types of unhealthy eating habits. Practicing mindful eating gives us the strength and skills we need to deal with such impulses. Instead of doing things at the whim of our instincts, techniques of mindful eating will put us in charge of our responses.

MINDFUL EATING AND WEIGHT LOSS

The majority of weight loss programs do not have a long-term effect. It has been seen that almost eighty-five percent of obese people who lost weight returned to or exceeded their original weight in the span of a few years. Weight gain and weight regain after losing weight successfully have been linked to eating in response to food cravings, external eating, emotional eating, and binge eating. Chronic exposure to stress can also play a significant role in obesity caused due to overeating.

Several studies agree that following the techniques of mindful eating; you can successfully change your eating behaviors and reduce your stress, which can lead to weight loss (Jennifer Daubenmier, 2011). An exploratory randomized controlled study was conducted on overweight and obese women to understand the effects of mindful eating.

Abdominal fat is promoted by the elevated secretion of cortisol as well as physiological distress. How abdominal fat gets affected by stress reduction interventions is unknown. Forty-seven obese or overweight women with a BMI of 31.2 were randomly assigned to a mindfulness intervention or a waitlist group that lasted four months, to understand the effects of mindfulness on stress eating. Cortisol-awakening response (CAR), weight, eating behavior, psychological distress, mindfulness, and abdominal fat pre- and post-treatment were assessed through this study. When compared to the control participants, the treatment participants were seen to have improved anxiety, mindfulness, and external-based eating behavior. Over time, the groups did not differ on abdominal fat, weight, or CAR. However, the obese control participants showed a stable CAR and gained weight, while the obese treatment participants showed no weight gain and a significant decrease in CAR. The reduction in abdominal fat was thus associated with improved mindfulness, CAR, and chronic stress.

Thus, this proof of concept study shows that the mindfulness program can improve CAR and eating patterns, which might help in the reduction of abdominal fat over time.

Another six-month-long study was conducted in which an average weight loss of twenty-six pounds was observed, without any weight regaining in the next three months

(Heather M. Niemeier, 2012). This pilot study examined the preliminary effectiveness and acceptability of a twenty-four-week intervention for weight loss among obese and over-weight people who reported problems with eating in response to thoughts and emotions.

By altering the way we think about food, any negative feeling that might be associated with eating can be replaced with positive emotions, improved self-control, and improved self-awareness. Mindful eating, thus, steers people away from making unhealthy choices. Your chances of successful long-term weight loss can also be increased by addressing the unwanted eating behaviors.

OTHER PHYSICAL BENEFITS OF MINDFUL EATING

Mindfulness meditation has shown to help reduce heart rate, blood pressure, cortisol levels as well as stress levels. A journal known as 'Obesity' published in October 2016 based on Daubenmier's research shows that mindful eating can improve our overall health. According to Daubenmier's research, it can reduce the ratio of HDL (good) cholesterol to triglycerides, which lowers the risk of heart diseases (Jennifer Daubenmier P. J., 2016). The study also suggests that eating mindfully can help control blood sugar levels, which might be possible because of the reduced consumption of sugary foods. Improved blood sugar control and improved cardiovascular health can help avoid Type 2 diabetes as well as health problems.

Another research led by Daubenmier called 'Mindfulness' was published online on September 10th, 2019. This study showed that eating mindfully, along with mindful meditation, can improve our cardiovascular responses to stress. It can help relax your blood vessels during stressful events. Therefore, mindful eating can help us perform better in stressful situations and also contribute to improving heart health.

Call to Action:

In the week ahead, pick one meal per day to start to pay attention to how you feel before, during, and after your eating process. What thoughts do you have going into this meal? What are you feeling while you are eating? What tastes are you noticing? How do you feel after you've finished eating?

3

DEFINING PHYSICAL HUNGER VS. EMOTIONAL HUNGER

U nderstanding the difference between physical hunger and emotional hunger can be quite tricky. In this chapter, I will try to help you understand the differences between them and help you find more satisfying ways to feed your feelings.

WHAT IS PHYSICAL HUNGER?

When you eat to fulfill your body's nutritional requirements, it is known as physical hunger or true hunger. You eat in response to your need to fuel your body so that you can make it through the day. Whenever your body needs to refuel itself, it will send you cues in the form of fatigue, headache, stomach grumbling, lightheadedness, and so on. Moreover, almost all kinds of foods, including vegetables and other healthy products, sound good when you are physically hungry.

WHAT IS EMOTIONAL HUNGER?

We don't always consume food only when we're physically hungry. A majority of us turn to food to reward ourselves for hard work, stress relief, or comfort. Emotional hunger is characterized by the need to eat to fill chronic or immediate emotional needs. When we are emotionally hungry, we mostly tend to reach for comforting but unhealthy food, like sweets and junk food. You might swing by the drive-through after a hard day at work, order a pizza when you are lonely or bored or eat a pint of ice cream when you're feeling sad.

Emotional eating involves using food to satisfy your emotional needs instead of filling your stomach. You eat to make yourself feel better. However, you should understand that emotional eating does not fix your on-going challenges or dilemmas. It can make you feel worse.

Here are some tips to help you understand whether you are an emotional eater:

- Do you feel out of control or powerless when you are around food?
- Do you feel like food is your friend?

- Does food make you feel safe?
- Do you usually eat until you're completely stuffed?
- Do you eat as a reward?
- Do you eat to soothe and calm yourself when you're anxious, bored, mad, sad, etc.?
- Do you continue to eat even when you're full or when you're not hungry?
- Do you tend to eat more when you feel stressed?

If your answer to any of these is yes, then you've already faced emotional hunger in your life without even realizing it.

DIFFERENCE BETWEEN HUNGER AND APPETITE

Before we move on to the difference between emotional hunger and physical hunger, I want to discuss the terms hunger and appetite, mainly because you will often find people use them interchangeably even though they have separate meanings attached to them. Itis elementary to lose touch with the cues of hunger and fullness in a culture that is obsessed with food and diet. However, once you understand the difference between these two terms, tuning into your satiety will become easier.

On its own, appetite is a good thing. If you have a healthy

appetite, it usually suggests that your body will get the required nutrients. However, it can become very easy for you to allow your appetite to take over your better judgment, which can result in obesity and over-eating. Reminding yourself about the differences between hunger and appetite can help you maintain a balanced attitude towards eating and food.

While hunger is your physiological need to eat, appetite can be defined as your desire to eat. When you're hungry, your body tells you to eat through several internal cues. Cues such as rumbling stomach growls are known as hunger pangs. Hunger is instinctive, and it cannot be controlled. When your stomach is empty, and the level of glucose in your blood drops below a certain point, a hormone known as ghrelin is secreted by the cells in your GI tract, as we talked about previously. This hormone signals your brain to increase the secretion of gastric acid and GI motility to prepare your body to start eating. This simply means that ghrelin starts to make you hungry.

Appetite, on the other hand, occurs as a coordinated effort between your stomach and your brain. You desire to eat food because of various external cues. It is not necessarily caused by your psychological need to eat. You can develop an appetite even by the mere thought of food. Your mouth might start to water, and you can practically feel the textures and taste the food on your palate when you feast your eyes on a delectable and delicious plate of food. However, unlike hunger, you cannot ignore your appetite. Moreover, your brain profoundly influences a learned behavior with appetite, and you can also learn to alter and control your appetite levels.

Don't confuse appetite with emotional eating, though, because appetite results simply from hearing or smelling food. In contrast, emotional eating is when you reach out for food due to your overwhelming emotions.

DIFFERENCE BETWEEN EMOTIONAL HUNGER AND PHYSICAL HUNGER

Using food occasionally as a reward, a pick-me-up, or to celebrate is not really a bad thing. However, when eating becomes your basic emotional coping mechanism, resulting in an impulse to eat whenever you feel bored, exhausted, lonely, angry, upset, or stressed. You can get stuck in a cycle that is unhealthy and never addresses the real problem or feeling.

You can never fulfill your emotional hunger with food. Even though eating might feel good at the moment, the feelings which led you to eat will still be present. Moreover, the unnecessary calories that you consumed may cause you to feel worse than you did before. You beat yourself up for not having more willpower and messing up.

Adding to the problem, you stop learning about healthier and better methods to manage your emotions. You start feeling more powerless over both your feelings and food, and you have a more difficult time trying to manage your weight. However, you can positively make changes, no matter how powerless you feel over your feelings and food. You can learn healthier methods to manage your emotions, conquer cravings, avoid triggers, and finally put an end to the cycle of emotional eating.

You should first learn how to differentiate between physical hunger and emotional hunger before you can break free from the emotional eating cycle. If you use food to deal with your feelings on a daily basis, it will be trickier than it sounds to recognize these differences, however, not impossible. The biggest problem with emotional hunger is that when it strikes, it can be so powerful and overwhelming that you can easily confuse it with physical hunger.

Here are some clues that can help you differentiate between emotional hunger and physical hunger:

- **Emotional hunger feels urgent** – While physical hunger comes on gradually, emotional hunger hits you in an instant and tends to feel immediate and overwhelming. You will feel like you have to eat right now to satisfy your hunger and get that instant feeling of satisfaction. On the other hand, with physical hunger, the urge to eat does not feel so extreme, nor does it demand prompt satisfaction unless you haven't had food for a long time.

- **Emotional hunger is not satisfied even when you're full –** With emotional hunger, your satiety levels are never met, and you keep wanting to eat more and more. You often tend to continue eating until you're uncomfortably stuffed. With physical hunger, however, you don't need to be stuffed. You will feel satiated (satisfied) once you've eaten, and your stomach is full.

- **Emotional hunger craves particular comfort foods –** Emotional hunger never makes you reach out for a salad or a green smoothie. Unless, of course, you are feeling contentment or peace at that moment, and in that case, that could lead you to choose something that is considered healthier. Instead, when you're emotionally hungry, you may end up craving sugary snacks or junk foods that will give you an instant rush. It will make you feel like your hunger can be satisfied only with a pizza or ice cream, and nothing else can fulfill it. Almost everything – including healthy foods, like vegetables – sounds good when you are physically hungry.

- **Emotional hunger can result in shame, guilt, or regret** – When you eat to fulfill your physical hunger, you're simply giving your body what it needs. Therefore, it's unlikely that you'll feel ashamed or guilty because of it. However, when you're eating because of the overwhelming feelings in your mind, you might feel guilty after you eat because you know it's not because of nutritional reasons.

- **Emotional hunger is not situated in the stomach** – When you're emotionally hungry, you are more focused on specific smells, tastes, and texture. You feel your hunger as an intense craving that you cannot get out of your head. In physical hunger, it's usually the pang in your stomach, your growling belly, or other hunger cues that make you feel hungry.

- **Emotional hunger often results in mindless eating** – When you eat because of your physical hunger, you are usually more aware of what you're eating. When your emotions drive your hunger, you can eat an entire pint of ice cream or a whole bag of chips without even realizing it or enjoying it.

HOW CAN YOU OVERCOME EMOTIONAL EATING WITH MINDFULNESS?

Often without us even realizing it, meals tend to become a form of self-medication for managing negative emotions. Recently, researchers have started viewing emotional eating as a response to both positive and negative moods (Gemma López-Guimerà, 2014). The concept of emotional eating is not as simple as it seems, and the latest studies reveal that it might reflect disregard of negative affect to episodic overeating, learned cue reactivity, and lack of control. In this respect, the way by which emotional eating is now measured might reflect that disinhibited eating is followed by 'over concern' or 'worry.' In the context of weight gain, it is crucial to study emotional eating and address it through mindfulness intervention as it results in poor outcomes in weight-loss interventions. In standard weight loss behavioral treatments, non-emotional eaters are almost twice as likely to reach the goal of ten percent weight reduction.

Behavioral interventions for weight loss do not have much scope for decreasing emotional eating. This is because they don't address the particular issues like how emotional eaters use their food to regulate emotions. Approaches that use mindfulness techniques have the potential to address this issue as they can produce beneficial outcomes by the modification of emotional regulation. Cross-sectional evidence proves that experiential avoidance acts as a mediator between emotional eating and negative behavior. Evidence also indicates that mindfulness is related to healthier eating. This association operates because of greater acceptance connected to self-compassion. Tolerance and acceptance of negative emotions are facilitated by mindfulness meditation. Mindfulness-based stress reduction (MBSR) program, devised by Kabat-Zinn, is the most widely used approach to mindfulness (R. S. Crane, 2016).

According to the American Psychological Association, almost twenty-seven percent of adults admitted that they eat to deal with stress, and another thirty-four percent of adults who admitted to overeating and eating unhealthy foods due to stress said their behavior is a habit. Research has revealed that mindfulness can turn food into a pleasure rather than an escape.

Psychologist Jean Kristeller says that by practicing mindfulness, we can identify the differences between real and emotional hunger and satiety. It inserts a moment of choice between our urge to eat something and eating it. It helps to bring our attention to every aspect of food, thereby help us change our attitudes and bodies.

CAUSES OF EMOTIONAL EATING

Emotional eating can be anything beginning with relationship struggles to health issues, financial worries to work stress. It can affect both men and women. However, various studies show that emotional eating is more prevalent in women than in men.

If you want to overcome emotional eating, work on identifying the triggers that are making you resort to this in the first place. Here are some of the most common factors that can cause emotional eating:

- **Stress** – Have you ever noticed that you get hungry when you're under any pressure? It is no longer just in your mind. When you're in extremely stressful situations, as often happens in our fast-paced and chaotic world, the stress hormone, cortisol, is released in high quantities by your body. Cortisol triggers cravings for foods – like sweet, salty, and fried foods – that will give you a burst of pleasure and energy. You are more likely to turn to emotional eating due to an increase in stress in your daily life.
- **Feelings of emptiness or boredom** – Do you eat as a way to fill up the gap in your life, to relieve boredom, or give yourself something to do? You

feel empty, unfulfilled, and feel as if eating is the way you can occupy your time and your mouth. It fills you up at the moment and distracts you from the dissatisfaction with your life and underlying feelings of purposelessness.

- **Keeping your emotions stuffed** – Food can be a way in which you can temporarily 'stuff down' or silence your shame, resentment, loneliness, anxiety, sadness, fear, anger, and other uncomfortable emotions. You can avoid the hard feelings that you don't want to feel by numbing yourself with food.

- **Social influences** – Eating a meal with other people is a great way to reduce stress. However, it can also result in overeating. It is effortless to overindulge just because everyone else is eating or because the food is just there. Nervousness can also cause you to overeat in certain social situations. You could also be encouraged to overeat by your friends and family, and it might seem to be easier if you went along with everyone else.

- **Childhood habits** – Your childhood habits related to food are often carried over into adulthood. Did your parents give you sweets when you were sad? Did they take you out for pizza when you got good marks? Or, did they reward your good

behavior with ice cream? Your eating habits could
be driven by nostalgia when you become an adult.

You can probably recognize yourself in at least some of the above descriptions. However, be even more specific about the reason why you're eating emotionally. Keeping an emotional eating diary to keep track of your food and moods is one of the best ways to understand the patterns behind why you're eating emotionally.

Pause for a moment every time you overeat or feel the urge to eat your comfort food and try to understand what triggered that urge. If you think back, you might identify the upsetting event that started the cycle of emotional eating. One example of this was within my upbringing. My parents kept soda and ice cream in our home at all times. To this day, it's essential for me not to keep these items around, because I would have a hard time not having some of these every day. I recognize that some of the ways I was brought up have caused some issues within my journey as an adult. If you feel you want to keep a diary for a time; jot everything down in your emotional eating diary: the food that you wanted to eat or ate, the event that upset you, your feelings before you ate, your emotions while you were eating, and your feelings after you've finished eating.

You'll notice that a pattern has developed over time. Maybe

you stress eat whenever you attend family gatherings or whenever you're on a deadline. Or perhaps you always end up overeating after spending time with a particular friend. Once you have successfully identified the triggers that cause you to overeat, you can start identifying healthier ways to manage your feelings.

WAYS TO FIGHT EMOTIONAL EATING

You won't be able to control your habits of emotional eating in the long term if you don't understand how to deal with your emotions. Diets tend to fail as they provide logical nutritional advice that only works if you can control your eating habits. However, when emotions hijack the process and demand an instant payoff with food, diets generally don't work.

If you want to stop emotional eating, you can work to find other methods by which you can satisfy yourself emotionally. Although understanding the triggers, patterns, and cycle of emotional eating is a huge first step, it is not enough to stop it. To find other alternatives to food that can guide you towards emotional fulfillment, will be the winning action.

Look for Other Methods to Deal With Your Stress

The first step towards fighting emotional eating is by

finding a new way to deal with negative emotions. You could do this by trying to relax and decompress from the day for a few minutes by reading a book or writing in a journal. To find the method that works best for you, try to experiment with different activities as it could take some time for you to be able to shift your attention from reaching for food to engaging in other methods of stress relief.

Start a Food Diary

To better identify the triggers that result in emotional eating, you can start keeping a log of everything you eat and the time when you eat them. You can note them down in a notebook or use technologies like the MyFitnessPal app.

Even though it might be challenging, try to note down everything you eat, however small or big it might be. Also, try to include the emotions that you're feeling at that moment. Your food diary could also be very helpful if you choose to seek professional help regarding your eating habits. This can often require a considerable slow down in activities and a decluttering of schedule to create space for this action. It's not easy, however, totally worth it!

Try Meditation

Several studies support that emotional eating and binge eating disorders can be treated by mindfulness meditation (Shawn N. Katterman, Mindfulness meditation as an intervention for binge eating, emotional eating, and weight loss: A systematic review, 2014).

Fourteen studies that investigated mindfulness meditation as the main intervention and assessed weight change, emotional eating, or binge eating were reviewed using the PRISMA method. The results indicated that mindfulness meditation effectively reduces emotional eating and binge eating in populations that engage in this behavior.

You can do simple deep breathing meditations almost anywhere. Just sit in a quiet environment, try to focus on your breathing, and slowly breathe in and out of your nose. When I used to work in an office setting, it was quite easy for me to be able to turn my chair in a position that wasn't facing anyone. I was able to take a 2-minute moment to myself, with eyes closed. You may not have the same opportunity; however, this can be something to try at home if you are unable to do this at work. If you want to see free guided meditations, you can browse sites like YouTube. For example, you can follow 'Guided Meditation for Anxiety & Stress' by Jason Stephenson, who has over four million views. It has a series of visualization and breathing exercises that take place for more than thirty minutes.

Try Exercising

Some people find relief by regularly exercising. A quick yoga routine or a walk or jog around the block can help you in several emotional situations.

A study was conducted to examine whether yoga could increase the level of mindfulness in healthy individuals (Danielle V. Shelov, 2009).

Forty-six volunteers were randomly assigned to a waitlist control group or a yoga intervention group for eight weeks to conduct the study. The Freiburg Mindfulness Inventory (FMI) was used to assess the levels of mindfulness pre and post-yoga. The results indicated that there was a significant increase in overall mindfulness in the yoga group participants. There was also an increase in their insightful understanding, accepting and open attitudes towards various experiences, and attention to the present moment.

Thus, the study revealed that yoga intervention could be a viable model for enhancing the levels of mindfulness in a healthy population. It also suggested that yoga could be used as prevention for the development of negative emotions like depression and anxiety. The participants of the control group also reported a moderate increase in mindfulness and insightful understanding.

Eat a Healthy Diet

It is vital to ensure that you eat enough nutrients so that you can fuel your body. Although it might be hard to differentiate between physical and emotional hunger, eating well throughout the day can help make it easier for you to identify when you're eating out of stress, sadness, or boredom.

If you're still having trouble, it's recommended that you try having healthy snacks that are low in fats and calories like plain popcorn, vegetables, and fresh fruits.

Although I stated in chapter 1 that mindful eating still allows you to eat whatever you want and while this is still true, it's also essential to be eating nutritious foods, and help us thrive.

Pay Attention to Volume

Try to avoid grabbing a whole pint of ice cream or other foods to snack on without paying attention to the amount. You can try mindful eating habits like choosing small plates and counting out portions to help you with portion control. After you've finished eating one serving, wait for some time before reaching out for another. In the meantime, you can try other techniques, like deep breathing, to relieve stress.

Throw Common Offenders Out of Your Cupboard

You should consider donating or trashing sweet or calorie-filled, high-fat foods, such as ice creams, chocolate, chips, etc. That might feel a bit extreme, and if so, enjoy them to the fullest! Keeping such foods that you crave out of reach during the moments of strife can help you break the cycle of emotional eating. It is also advised to postpone any trips to the grocery stores when you are feeling down.

Banish Distractions

You might find yourself using your phone or watching the computer or TV while you're eating. The next time you find yourself in such patterns, try putting down your phone or switching off the TV. If you focus on the level of your hunger, your food, and the bites you're taking, you might be able to identify whether you're eating emotionally.

Seek Support

Try to avoid isolation when you're sad or anxious. Even a quick phone call to a family member or friend can immensely improve your mood.

Call to Action:

Don't move too fast into this one. Be sure to complete the first two calls to action before moving forward. In thinking about the week ahead, pick one meal this week to pause before and look at your food.

- Observe the colors and the look of the meal.
- Pick up your food. What words would you use to

describe your food? Notice the aroma of your food. How does this make you feel?

- Take one bite. Chew it slowly. Notice the sensations on your tongue. Pay attention to salivation. Is it sweet, savory, salty? After chewing slowly, swallow and notice the way it feels going down your esophagus.

- Take one small bite and notice the sound of your teeth as you eat. You are introducing more mindful moments!

- Yes, these action points are repetitive. Remember that bringing these mindful moments in can be challenging. Practicing over and over can help solidify the action. This is why I am taking you through the same steps week after week. You can do this!

4

LIVING OUT MINDFUL EATING DAY TO DAY

M indful eating is a practice that takes time and is all about focusing on the present. You might think that you have to incorporate the last call to action into every meal, but there are so many ways to practice mindful eating every day. This chapter will mainly focus on how we can start instilling mindfulness in our day to day life. Practicing mindfulness day to day means including moments that will help us realize that we can live more intentionally. It can also help hone the skills that can help manage not just our weight but even more. Mindful eating also involves bringing in behavioral changes that can help us fight sleep disorders, depression, as well as chronic pain.

When we start eating mindfully, we have to slow down and start noticing our hunger levels and our emotions. This helps us taste the food properly in our mouth and eat when we're hungry. Moreover, we can practice mindful eating regardless of our eating style because it's about how we eat and not about what we eat. This means that you can learn the techniques of mindful eating regardless of whether you're gluten-free, vegan, or paleo. Lastly, eating mindfully focuses on improving our relationship with food. Eating mindfully, of course, helps break the cycle of emotional eating by introducing new practices.

EAT SLOWLY AND MINDFULLY

The five basic tenets of mindful eating are sitting, slowing down, savoring, simplifying, and smiling. With some practice, these tenets can become your second nature before you even know it. It is recommended that you sit down when you eat. Even though it might sound easy, you'll be surprised to find out how often you eat standing, when you become more aware of this action. When compared to eating while sitting, it was found that people eat five percent more while standing.

Eating your food slowly is the next step to eating mindfully. When you eat slowly, you are more aware of the food that you are putting inside your mouth, and you automatically become aware of how much you are eating. You also start focusing on what the texture or color of the food is, all of which could be neglected entirely. A recent study showed how weight loss and better health can be achieved by mindfulness, and not by restricting or eating certain kinds of foods (Carolyn Dunn, 2018). The study showed how people became more aware of their bodies once they started practicing mindfulness. They even became more in tune with their satiety and hunger levels. The cravings gradually reduced, and the tendency to engage in eating practices as a reward also decreased.

Slowing down gives your brain time to contemplate every bite and also helps you break down the food. Slowing down is one of the best ways by which you can get your body and your mind to communicate on what you require for nutrition. You might often tend to overeat unconsciously. This overeating is because it takes almost twenty minutes for the satiation signal to reach your brain. However, when you slow down while eating, you are providing your body with the opportunity to catch up with your brain so that it can hear the signals and eat the correct amount. Therefore, if you want to eat slowly, you have to prepare for it.

- Start by creating a calm environment around you. When you are not disturbed or distracted, you are more likely to focus on the food that you put in your mouth. You can even listen to some calming music or light a scented candle and keep it on the table.

- Decrease as many distractions as you can. This also means that you should not eat and do other things, especially when you are at home. Keep your phone and any other gadgets away. Turn off the TV. You can do all of that at another time. Finish your meal in peace.

- If you have a habit of eating while standing in the kitchen, this could be worth changing because it is something that automatically speeds up the pace at which you eat.

- You can learn to appreciate every moment when you eat. Sit down and take a short pause. Take in some deep breaths, and if you have a tradition of saying grace, then do so. Or, you can at least be grateful for the food on your table and thank the person who made it.

- The next thing that you could focus on is food, its color, texture, and smell. Once you take a small mouthful, let the food stay in your mouth so that you can savor the taste. You can practice chewing the food for at least five times before you gulp it down. After every bite, take a pause of about ten seconds before you take another bite.

- During your meal, take a moment to assess your

hunger and satiety levels. Ask yourself whether you are still eating just to finish the food in front of you, or are you longing for sustenance. If you are eating with someone else, enjoy that person's company, but if you are someone who likes to eat in silence, you might try eating without someone eating with you.

- Lastly, try smiling between bites. Although it might sound a little weird, it might give you some time to assess whether you're genuinely satisfied.

CULTIVATE A MINDFUL KITCHEN

Rather than thinking about our snacks and meals proactively, we often eat mindlessly by eating at random places and times or wandering about searching through cabinets. Even though it slows us down, it also stops us from cultivating healthy environmental cues regarding what to eat and how much. It can also wire our brains about new cues for eating that may not be ideal.

Cultivating a mindful kitchen means caring for and organizing your kitchen space to promote healthy eating and nourishing gatherings. Think about the things you want to bring into your kitchen and where you want to keep it. Are healthy foods handy? What types of foods are in your sight? It can boost the health of your body as well as your mind. It will also help your mood, your sleep schedule, and help you eat at fixed times and places. This means sitting down at a table and keeping the food on a bowl or plate, using utensils and not your hands, and not eating out of a container. It can also help you to eat with other people. You are not only sharing your food and receiving some healthy connection, but it also lets you slow down and enjoy the conversation and the food even more. You can take cues from your dinner partner so as not to under or overeat because of emotions.

It's essential to be flexible when you're practicing mindful eating. You don't need to plan your meals down to every bite. Be aware that you might have to change your eating habits for different occasions or at different times of the year. However, when you plan, it's more likely that you will eat the right amount that your body requires at that moment, rather than overeating and regretting it later, or undereating and indulging later.

It is also not the wisest idea to go shopping when you're hungry. A psychological effect called 'moral licensing' revealed that shoppers who buy healthy foods first are more likely to head to the ice cream or alcohol section after that than those who don't. They seem to believe that everything will balance out, and they can spend it on less than ideal behaviors, like buying junk food. That's not to say you should never buy these types of foods. Going in hungry, though, can increase the odds of choosing foods that may not feel the greatest for your body.

HOW TO EAT MINDFULLY WHEN YOU ARE WITH OTHERS?

For many of us being surrounded by families, jobs, and various distractions, eating as mindfully as we do in a mindfulness course or on a retreat might not be realistic or possible. When we eat with our colleagues, family, and friends, they might not have the patience to eat with us while we take 5 minutes with every bite. Also, during the stress, craziness, and extra food of the holidays that stretch from Halloween to the New Year, we are more likely to eat mindlessly than mindfully. There are certain things that you can do to help yourself eat mindfully even in these situations –

- **Ground yourself** – When you sit down, make sure you are comfortable. If you are not, then it will lead to a feeling of uneasiness and anxiety, and one thing will lead to another where the end result would be you overeating because of social anxiety. Put yourself in situations that feel the best for you. If you need to, say no to the things that you feel you need to say no to. So, making yourself comfortable and grounding yourself is the first step to eating mindfully in public. Take a moment to quietly be thankful in your mind for this moment, and to take a silent breath.

- **Order first** – If the waiter comes to take the order, give your order first. Don't wait for someone else. You will notice that the tone of the table is often set by the person who orders first, so why not be that person yourself? In this way, you can listen to what your body truly needs from a nutritional point of view and order that item instead of being swayed by others. One of the core concepts of both intuitive and mindful eating is that you have to listen to what your body is trying to tell you and eat accordingly without worrying about what others may be ordering.

- **Order what you know** – Irrespective of when you order, try to stick with something that you already know. In this way, you will know what to expect, and this can help you use your mental energy to communicate with the people around you instead of examining the food. This will ensure that even if you are not feeling the food and focusing on every ingredient in your mouth, you can enjoy it. In turn, you will also be able to socialize with those around you.

- **Put the fork down from time to time** – One

of the best things about eating with company is that you can increase your time to eat the food by engaging in conversation with others. When you are eating, and you have food in your mouth, eat and think about the taste. You may find this challenging if you are also trying to listen to conversation; however, use your best judgment here. When you are talking, enjoy the moment and put down the fork. In turn, when someone else starts talking, you can take the fork back up again and take another mouthful.

CONNECT WITH YOUR FOOD MORE DEEPLY

In recent years all of us have become more disconnected from our food unless you are a farmer or a hunter-gatherer. Most of us don't even think about where our food comes from beyond the supermarket packaging. However, eating can provide us with excellent opportunities to connect more deeply with the elements of the natural world and to each other.

If you take a moment to consider all the people who are involved in making the meal that is in front of you, you start to see all of the blessings around you as well. Starting from the person who cooked it, to those who stocked the shelves in the supermarket, to those who planted the raw materials and harvested them and those who supported them, it's not difficult to feel interconnected as well as grateful. When you sit down to eat whatever you're eating, be mindful of all the elements like the water, soil, etc. that were required for its creation. You can also reflect on the recipes that were generously shared by your friends or your ancestors who brought it from a distant place, and all cultural traditions that brought you to your meal.

So the next time you visit a restaurant with your young children, talk about the whole process of bringing food to the plate. Talk about where it came from, how it was grown, who stocked it, and who prepared it and brought it to the tables. It can be a learning process to share with your children. A crucial moment for your kids to find out where food comes from and how it showed up on the plate in front of them. Also, it can be a fantastic moment for you to get connected with the food you are eating. Mindful moments don't have to be complicated, thank goodness!

DON'T MULTITASK

If you would like to build the habit of mindful eating from day to day, an excellent place to start is to move past multitasking and focus on doing just one activity at a time. Multitasking while eating results in not being able to listen to the needs and wants of your body. When you are distracted, it becomes more difficult for you to listen to your body's signals about food and other needs. One of the most common examples of mindless eating and multitasking is when you keep eating popcorn while watching movies in the theatre. The tub of popcorn you came in with is finished before the movie gets over, making you question who ate all the popcorn.

With your next meal, try to single-task and just eat. Make it an event to slow down and make your mealtime the center focus. Instead of sitting in front of the TV, try conversing with the people whom you're sharing a meal.

When you are thinking about your to-do list and eating at the same time, you definitely would not be able to think deeply about the two things at the same time. And so, this increases your chance to overeat. There was a research conducted in the year 2013, which showed that people are more likely to engage in overeating when they multitask (Reine C. van der Wal, 2013). To feel full, your body needs to have an idea about taste perception. Still, when you focus on doing other things, your body is not able to focus on the five tastes. That is how your brain signals you to resort to overeating.

TAKE THE RAISIN EXERCISE

Remember how I asked you to try meditation for mindful eating? Well, there is a raisin exercise under the guidance of Kabat-Zinn that you could try (Kabat-Zinn, 1991).

If you aren't a big fan of raisins, try this with a peanut or something similar:

- Take one raisin and place it on the table in front of you. Don't take a bunch of raisins but only one.
- Now, you have to expand your imagination power and think of yourself as someone who has come to this planet out of nowhere, and you know nothing of this place. You don't remember any experiences from Earth, and everything is new to you. First, take a couple of deep breaths and then bring your mind to a relaxed state.
- Take the raisin in your hands and think about the weight of the raisin.
- Examine the raisin's texture by touching different parts of it – the ridges, the dull parts, and the shiny parts. You have to examine it as if it were a very strange object that you are looking at for the first time.
- Then, smell the raisin and think about how it smells. Take note of how you react to the smell.

- After that, put the raisin between two fingers and roll it to understand its stickiness and whether it makes any sound. You will slowly understand how you feel about the raisin.
- Now, take the raisin and place it between your lips. Don't touch it with your tongue. Simply put it between your lips and notice what happens in your mind and body.
- Let the raisin go inside your mouth. Keep rolling it around in your mouth without chewing it. Do you salivate, or do you get any taste?
- Now, take one bite into the raisin. Don't bite more than once. Take a mental note of how you feel.
- After this, chew the raisin slowly and try to feel the reaction in your body.
- Keep chewing until the point where the raisin becomes near liquid, and then you can swallow it.
- Once you have swallowed the raisin, revisit the experience in your mind, and think about how you felt.

Mindful eating is going to look precisely like the raisin activity. You are enjoying each moment one by one and then slowly moving on to the next level. You have full intention to focus on the process of eating. All of this makes you truly aware of the food you are eating.

This may have felt like a daunting or unfamiliar process; however, it's good to remember that the more often you practice mindful eating, the easier this experience will feel. This experiment does not mean that this is how you will approach every mindful moment. It's simply a chance to go through a powerful mindful experiment.

UNDERSTAND YOUR MOTIVATIONS

Are you eating foods that are nutritionally healthy or foods that are emotionally comforting? If you are to strike a balance between these two, it can be really tricky. Think about the raisin activity once again – did it seem appealing to you even before you tried it? The raisin activity is potent for several reasons. One of the main reasons is that when we slow down and consume healthy foods like fruits and vegetables, we tend to enjoy it more than the story associated with healthy foods.

When we practice consuming healthier foods, we become more inclined towards enjoying healthy foods and less inclined towards binging on comfort foods. This ultimately helps us find more foods mentally and physically satisfying as opposed to only a few.

You also have to ask yourself whether you are ready for this change or not. Walking on the path of mindful eating is not a cakewalk, and you can do it successfully only when you truly feel that your life needs a change. When we start to introduce new methods into our lives, we need to be ready for a change so we can persevere through the hard parts.

Call to Action:

After completing the last challenge, if you find that you are eating a meal with electronics, pick a couple of times this week where you could practice eating mindfully by turning off electronics, really engaging in the eating process, and eating slowly. Put the fork down between bites or connect with those you love.

5

STOP COUNTING CALORIES

I f you learned that a handful of carrots had the same amount of calories as a handful of chips, which one would you choose to eat as your next snack? You would probably choose the second option, right? You might wonder why you eat carrots if chips have the same amount of calories and taste better than carrots? Calories are, however, simply an indicator of the amount of energy present in a particular food. They don't tell us anything about the nutrition level or the overall quality of the food. Before obesity turned into an epidemic, people used to eat food for the proteins that could help maintain their nails and hair, or the vitamins that could ward off diseases. To focus on calories only, we seem to have forgotten about several important aspects of our food.

WHY COUNTING CALORIES DOESN'T WORK?

Even though counting calories might make us aware of our average energy intake, it most likely won't result in a sustainable change in behavior. This is because our focus is on quantifying our eating habits rather than focusing on the process of eating.

A calorie can be defined as the amount of energy necessary to increase the temperature of a gram of water by 1 degree Celsius. From the perspective of physics, this means that a calorie is just a unit of energy. Regardless of the source, a calorie is a calorie thermochemically, but not metabolically. However, calories are not equal to metabolism. This suggests that the focus is not on quantity but on the quality of the food. Those are two separate concepts.

To be honest, the human body was not designed to be filled with high amounts of sodium or sugar, chemical preservatives, and other artificial products. All these are different components of processed foods. You might be wondering how we can change this then. Well, we can improve this by starting to focus on the process of eating mindfully.

In today's busy world, all of us are mentally overtaxed and pressed for time. Family obligations and career can immensely affect our capacity for taking on an extra thing, whether it involves making space for self-care or lack of time, or both. It's not a surprise that most of us look for instant fixes for losing weight. A good part of the time, the growing stress of life, along with the sedentary demands of the office, can lead to weight gain, but it goes unnoticed until it gets too late. There's a creeping feeling of fatigue even before you know it. It can decrease our motivation for activities that burn calories.

Even though counting calories has been around us for a long time, it is not easy to lose weight. This struggle is because re-training our minds and bodies can be a complicated process, and we might think we don't have the tools required to do it.

For some people, the answer to this could be using diet and fitness apps on their computers and smartphones to count and keep track of their calorie intake. This popular age-old technique seems to be a good idea for people who are dieting for the first time as well as for more seasoned dieters as it is accessible, relatively compatible with most lifestyles, easy to manage, and free in many respects. It can give you a clear picture of the trends or habits that you might need to refine.

Logging calories can also bring awareness to your choices regarding food. It might be necessary for some time. However, in the long run, moving away from counting and logging calories can help free us to practice mindful eating, listen to our bodies, and be more in tune with the foods that are filling as well as nutritious.

REASONS NOT TO COUNT CALORIES ANYMORE

Counting calories won't be sustainable if it turns into a strict rule-based method by which you start policing your diet. Here are some reasons why counting calories might not necessarily be the healthiest way to choose foods:

Not All Calories Are Similar

A calorie is just a unit of energy. Your body either holds calories as fat or uses them to perform tasks like keeping your organs functioning or regulating your body temperature. The kind of calories you consume determines whether your body stores the calories you eat or uses them. When you consume processed foods like crackers and chips, the calories from them are most likely to be stored. These differ from the calories from whole foods, like vegetables and fruits, which will be utilized.

Healthy Might Be Rich In Calories

You might be surprised to learn that avocados have almost three hundred calories. However, if you didn't eat your favorite avocado toast due to the number of calories present in it, you could be missing out on all the antioxidants, good fats, potassium, fiber, and folate that are present in it. This is also true for several other high-calorie and healthy foods, including quinoa, olive oil, and walnuts. While you may not want to eat a whole avocado in one sitting, it's a fantastic way to get in a healthy fat!

How can you make an educated decision regarding food if you have to make counting calories a part of your decision-making? Well, checking the nutrient density of the food can help you with that. Foods that are rich in nutrients have more of the good stuff, such as phytochemicals, healthy fats, proteins, minerals, and vitamins packed into every calorie. For instance, sweet potatoes with around a hundred calories have more nutrients like Vitamin C, Vitamin A and fiber compared to a hundred calories worth of white bread.

According to Emily Kyle (M.S., C.D.N., R.D.N.), two separate food items can have the same number of calories. Still, they might contain different amounts of essential nutrients that are required by your body to function properly every day. She says that we might miss out on the nutrients that actually matter the most if we keep our focus solely on the number of calories.

A large portion of people tend to believe that foods labeled as 'low calorie' is good for them. This, however, is not true. For instance, let's assume that you wanted to have a smoothie made of chia seeds, spinach, banana, and straw-berry for breakfast. You then visit a grocery store and see that you can instead buy a breakfast drink that has a lower number of calories than the smoothie that you wanted to prepare. So you drink the breakfast drink instead. However, while your homemade smoothie has unprocessed vegetables and fruits, this is not true of all store-bought smoothies. The store-bought breakfast drink has ingredients like sucralose, canola oil, polydextrose, and maltodextrin – all of which can be bad for your health. Thus, you need to understand that just because a food has fewer calories, it doesn't always suggest that you should put it inside your body.

The Two Thousand Calorie Diet Is Unrealistic

The two thousand calorie diet suggests that one person should consume two thousand calories a day in order to stay healthy. As the number is an average, women tend to assume they require less than two thousand calories, and men tend to assume they require some more. However, it turns out that the number is completely made up.

The FDA used the research conducted by the USDA to get their information while they were trying to understand what the average daily intake of calories should be. In these stud-ies, children reported consuming around eighteen hundred to twenty-five hundred calories per day. Men reported consuming around two thousand to three thousand calories every day, and women reported consuming around sixteen hundred to twenty-five hundred calories every day. The FDA used this data to decide that the average number of calories an individual should consume in a day is 2,350. Some people, however, thought that the amount was very high and could encourage people to overeat. Therefore, they made the decision to reduce the number to two thousand calories per day.

Marion Nestle, Professor at the New York University in the Department of Nutrition, Food Studies, and Public Health, says that an average non-obese adult female requires around twenty-four hundred calories every day while an adult male requires around three thousand calories every day to maintain stable body weight. However, these amounts can still change from person to person, depending on the amount of physical activity, weight, and height. It's all about finding the number that is right for you, and this might require experimenting if you are someone who may end up counting calories for a time.

Calorie budgets are going to vary from person to person. One woman who is 68 and already weighs in at 140 pounds, may need a totally different budget than another woman who may weigh in at 195 pounds who is 28 years old. These varying descriptions will define quite a bit about what budget she might keep and what foods she might consume.

Calorie Counting Can Take All the Enjoyment Away From Eating

One of the greatest pleasures in life is being able to share a meal with our friends, family, and loved ones. Counting the calories in each bite you take can take away all the pleasure. It can eventually result in a bad relationship with food. It can turn something that you considered as an ally into an arch-enemy – something that you'll need to control and subdue.

You Can't Accurately Count the Number of Calories You're Consuming

It is a prevailing theory that gain or loss in weight = calories in or calories out. However, there is no way of accurately measuring how many calories you're consuming unless you take everything you consume to a laboratory. In one study, a woman reported that she was consuming only one thousand calories every day. However, when her food was measured with the help of a calorie counting machine, it was revealed that she was consuming more than three thousand calories per day.

This is primarily because of inaccurate food labels. The calorie count on food labels is allowed to vary up to twenty percent from the real number as per USDA laws. This issue suggests that your one hundred-calorie granola bar might have as many as 120 calories or as little as eighty calories, but there is no way by which you can know which one the real value is.

The calorie counts written on restaurant menus are also very inaccurate. A study revealed that the number of calories printed on the menus could be wrong by more than hundreds of calories. Researchers also revealed that food items that were thought to be less healthy, often had fewer calories than reported on the menu. In comparison, food items that were considered healthier often had more calories than that suggested on the menu.

Calorie Counting Fails to Make You Recognize Your Body's Signals

Every one of us was born with the ability to realize when we are hungry and when we are full. However, the problem is that these signals are subtle, and you need to have mindful concentration to recognize them. It is better to try to develop our goals by reconnecting with our bodies instead of relying on words and numbers indicated on the side of a package.

It Tends to Make You Hungry

Generally, you expect that you'll feel hungry when you're on a diet because you're eating less than what you're used to consuming. Due to this, you tend to feel hungry even after you've eaten, and your stomach is full. This might result in overeating, which is exactly what you want to avoid.

A research conducted by Health Cast revealed that the way a food item is explained can influence how hungry you might feel after you've eaten it. In this research, a chocolate and raspberry protein bar was given to a group of people. While they described it as a 'chocolate bar that is extremely yummy and tasty having a raspberry chocolate core' to some people, to others, they described it as a 'new health bar'. They found that those people who had the bar described as a chocolate bar felt less hungry as compared to those who had it described as being healthy.

Another research conducted by sciencedirect.com, gave either a low-calorie drink or a high-calorie drink to ten non-calorie restricting women and ten calorie restricting women. They labeled some of the drinks wrong in a way that a low-calorie drink was labeled as high-calorie and vice versa. Although all the women felt fuller after consuming the high-calorie drink, hunger in women who were calorie-restricted was highly influenced by the label of the drink.

It Can Result In Eating Disorders

When people follow the motto 'Eat less, move more' to lose weight, they tend to significantly increase the amount of exercise they do and reduce the number of calories they consume. You are more likely to over-exercise compulsively if you are exercising with the sole purpose of burning calories. Compulsive over-exercise can result in overuse injuries as well as metabolic issues. This can eventually cause eating disorders.

Scott Parker, James J. Gray, and Sarah T. Hubbard professors at the American University in the Department of Psychology conducted several studies on individuals who compulsively over-exercised. They found that the exercises that were related to food showed more symptoms of low self-esteem, body dissatisfaction, eating disturbances, and obligatory exercise as compared to non-food-related exercisers.

It Can Cause Stress

According to research published by the U.S. National Library of Medicine National Institutes of Health, counting calories can cause significant stress issues. They observed four groups of participants in the study. In one control group, the participants didn't restrict or monitor their calorie intake, and in another restricting group, the participants followed a diet of twelve hundred calories per day and received pre-packaged meals. There was a monitored group in which the participants racked but didn't restrict their calorie intake. There was also a monitoring and restricting group in which the participants followed a diet of twelve hundred calories every day but had to plan their meals. They found that the participants who restricted their calorie intake had a higher level of the stress hormone cortisol. Even though they did not feel stressed, those who monitored their calories had higher perceived stress.

DO CALORIES MATTER FOR LOSING WEIGHT?

You might have heard that you need to burn more calories than you eat to lose weight. However, the equation for weight loss is a little more complicated. Daily activity and lifestyle, along with diet factors, can play a significant role in weight loss. For example, you might eat less throughout the day when you consume fats (like walnuts) that can help keep you full. This might also be true for low-fat versus full-fat dairy. Studies show that there's a link between decreased risk of obesity and reaching for higher-calorie, full-fat dairy. Moreover, several studies have also been conducted on how consuming a high-protein breakfast can help you feel full throughout the morning and help you eat less all day.

However, the total number of calories can make a difference if you aim to lose weight. Let's consider the avocado example once again. If a 130-pound adult female ate three avocados every day in addition to her regular diet, she would gain weight because of those extra nine hundred calories. Even though those calories were obtained from nutritious avocados rather than from ice cream and cakes. However, if some of the other three hundred calorie food items were replaced with other nutrient-rich foods, it might have helped keep her full for a longer time and prevent her from overeating later during the day. Therefore, losing or maintaining weight is a balancing act. Even though calories matter, the overall nutrient composition of the food also equally matters.

MAKING COUNTING CALORIES WORK FOR YOU

Taking a look at the big picture and shifting focus from counting calories to losing weight can immensely help with understanding the difference between weight loss, bone muscle, and water loss. It might also affect your basal metabolic rate because of the extra weight gain that occurs after the original weight returns. Your original weight almost always comes back when you solely rely on counting calories and don't follow the techniques that you need to stop it from coming back.

It's a strong reason to not solely rely on decreasing calorie intake and also exercise and consider nutrition. All of our bodies are different, and they respond differently. We process food, salt, water, and stress in different ways. What might work for a fit 20-year-old might not work for a 70-year-old person. What works for a 5k runner might not work for a pregnant woman. I would never prescribe a one set method for any person.

When we try new approaches without any guidance or support, we often fail at them and blame ourselves. Counting calories only work when paired with a proper exercise routine and a nutritious meal plan. These methods, when accompanied by adequate support, water intake, mental well-being, appropriate sleep, and small achievable wins, can contribute to new workable habits. This process will vary from person to person. I have personally coached people who find this process quite daunting, while others thrive. I am not going to tell you one way or another, to stop or to take part in this process, but instead to do what feels right for you. A lifestyle that is inspiring, rewarding, and doesn't make you deprived is an excellent way of approaching long-term weight loss.

Call to Action:

In the week ahead, if you are not counting calories, download a free app such as MyfitnessPal or Noom, and start logging. No matter how big or small a meal (think about those 5 M&M's or that healthy apple or those five beers), log it! Do it with enthusiasm for seven days. Consider the nutrition of each item. Consider your exercise for the week.

Consider the amount of water you are getting in. If seven days feels too daunting, start with just 2-3.

If you are already logging your food, consider your exercise for the week. Consider the amount of water you are getting in or the amount of sleep you are getting each night. What could use refining?

6

STRESS-BUSTING STRATEGIES

S tress can cause more than just mental side effects. It can play a huge role in impacting your emotions, your mental health, as well as your physical health. In fact, mental stress has several physical side effects, including weight loss. While some people experience weight loss, others may gain weight with added stress. In the first part of this chapter, I will be discussing the role stress plays in weight loss or weight gain while the other part will be about implementing stress relievers and recognizing when things are out of control versus when things are in our control.

CAN STRESS MAKE YOU GAIN WEIGHT?

Stress can result in weight gain. Your body releases many different hormones when it's under pressure. Your body has increased levels of cortisol during this time. Even though it serves a useful purpose when you're stressed, it can also have a domino effect in the other areas of your body. Cortisol provides you with some extra energy when it thinks your body might require it. However, this can increase your appetite, and you could end up eating more than you normally would.

Moreover, people who struggle with emotional eating don't always eat to nourish their bodies or when they're hungry, but also eat to satisfy their feelings. If you eat emotionally, it means you end up eating in response to your feelings of happiness, sadness, anger, or stress. When you're under stress, food can turn into comfort as you are not sure how to handle it. People suffering from chronic stress, improper hormonal balance, and emotional eating can also result in weight gain.

CAN STRESS CAUSE WEIGHT LOSS?

For some people, stress and weight loss go hand in hand. When they are under stress, they start to lose weight without even trying instead of gaining it. Although it might sound like a good idea when you have a few extra pounds and want to lose it, it's not.

Here are a few ways by which stress can result in weight loss:

- **Loss of appetite** – When you're going through a stressful situation, it can completely take over your mind. You might lose your appetite while trying to find a solution or worrying about the things that are happening and the things that could happen. When your mind is distracted by multiple factors, it becomes easy to forget that you have to eat. The anxiety you're experiencing might also make you not feel hungry at all. Eating could become the last thing you want to do, even if you know you have to eat. It could also be that you don't want to put anything in your mouth because no food sounds good or because you just feel a bit queasy.

- **Digestive issues** – Your body releases hormones to help you when you're under a lot of stress. Therefore, in stressful situations, it's natural for you to experience a fight or flight response. This fight or flight response can cause digestive issues. When your body is trying to give you the energy it requires for flight or fight response, it wants to burn as few calories as it can. This action, in turn, suggests that your body is not helping your digestive system to be on track. This can result in many problems such as stomach cramping, nausea, constipation, diarrhea, etc. Often when you have these symptoms, the last thing you might want to do is eat. The result can cause a loss of weight.

- **Increased metabolism –** Another result of the fight or flight experience is that it can increase your metabolism. This fight or flight response can result in an increased appetite. However, if your body is working overtime to provide you with energy by burning calories, but you're not increasing your eating, you can experience weight loss.

- **You move more –** Some people move a lot when they're stressed. They might keep tapping their fingers, shaking their knees while sitting in a chair, or pace around a room when they are worrying or trying to process the information in stressful situations. These additional movements, even if they're little, can burn extra calories. This could result in weight loss when you combine it with loss of appetite and increased metabolism.

WHEN SHOULD YOU BE CONCERNED?

When you're going through a stressful situation in life, it is essential that you pay close attention to things such as your weight gain or loss. In such circumstances, it's easy to get caught up and let such things go unnoticed. However, this is not the healthiest way to lose weight.

Check for these following symptoms if you are going through a stressful time and losing weight.

- Abusing substances
- Increased irritability
- Chest pains
- Frequent headaches
- Loss in about five percent body weight within six to twelve months even though you're not trying to lose weight.

CAN STRESS AFFECT LIFE EXPECTANCY?

Several studies have pointed out the fact that women tend to live longer than men. Even though biological factors and lifestyle play a major role in the gender gap, recent studies show that the gap becomes even smaller when stress is involved. Research published in *BMJ Open Journal* showed that heavy stress and the quality of life decrease life expectancy by more than two years in both men and women.

Studies conducted by the Finnish Institute of Health and Welfare predicted life expectancy by evaluating quality-of-life factors as well as traditional lifestyle risk factors. Data from over 38,000 participants between the age of twenty-five and seventy-four were studied to conduct this research. For thirty-year-old women experiencing chronic stress, their life expectancy was observed to be reduced by 2.3 years, and for men, it was reduced by 2.8 years. According to the research, experiencing little stress, but not more than the usual was associated with reduced hazards. This data suggested that individuals who believed that their stress level was neither more nor less than the others around them had a better life expectancy.

The researchers looked at four factors, including lifestyle and biological risk factors, medical history, socio-demographic background, and life satisfaction (stress). The most significant cause of decreased life expectancies included type 2 diabetes and smoking. It could reduce the expected age of death (EAD) by some more than five years in women and some more than six years in men.

TIPS TO RELIEVE STRESS

Even though biological stress is a relatively recent discovery identified and documented by endocrinologist Hans Selye in the late 1950s, symptoms of stress existed long before his discovery. Nowadays, almost seventy percent of adults in the US have reported feeling anxiety or stress daily.

Here are some tangible actions that you can take to reduce stress:

Breathe Through the Hard Moments

Mental stress signals your body to go into fight or flight mode by activating your sympathetic nervous system. Stress hormones are released during this reaction, and you might experience physical symptoms like constricted blood vessels, faster breathing, and increased heart rate.

Deep breathing exercises can help control your relaxation response by activating your parasympathetic nervous system. There are different kinds of deep breathing exercises, like paced respiration, belly breathing, abdominal breathing, and diaphragmatic breathing. The aim of these exercises is to completely focus on your breathing and making it deeper and slower. Your belly rises and your lungs expand fully when you deeply breathe in through your nose.

This movement also helps you to feel more peaceful by slowing your heart rate.

Take a break for five minutes and focus on your breathing. Sit straight with your hand on your stomach and your eyes closed. Slowly breathe in through your nostrils, try to feel the breath start in your belly and make its way towards your head. Then exhale through your mouth. Taking just a minute or two to breathe can help you regulate your nervous system. There are some fantastic apps like Calm and Headspace, that can help you with your breathing or meditative moments.

Laugh

Find a way to get a good laugh in. You could try spending time with your friends and family, watching a funny TV show, going to see a comedy show or some other way. When you're laughing, it'll be hard to feel anxious. Laughter and happiness have an amazing effect on our well-being and can also help relieve stress:

- Relieving tension by relaxing our muscles.
- Relieving our stress responses.

It can also improve your mood and immune system in the long term.

A research conducted on people who have cancer revealed that individuals who participated in the laughter intervention group experienced better stress relief than those who were only distracted (Mary P Bennett, 2003).

You can also try to rewire your brain to be happier by recounting your laughter moments throughout the day. Following this gratitude exercise, you need to recount at least a few moments of laughter every night. This exercise can make you feel happy about yourself and relieve some of the stressful moments.

Another method of rewiring your brain to be happier is by taking time every day to write and reflect. You don't even have to write down sentences; you can just jot down random words, doodle, scribble, or whatever comes to your mind. You only need to have the intention to reflect and jot something down on a piece of paper. Recent studies have shown that individuals who spent at least 20 minutes to jot down their experiences had a drastic improvement in their happiness. Journaling can thus, benefit your mental health in many ways.

Say No More Often

Although all stressors are not under your control, some are. Think about the situations in which you have the power to say no, which could help slow you down a bit. Try to take control of the circumstances that are causing you stress, and you can change. Ask yourself if now could be an appropriate time to schedule a decluttering, just as you would do with your closets and junk drawer from time to time. Could it be time to sift through some 'junk' in your life, and say no?

It is particularly true if you find yourself juggling several responsibilities and taking on so much that it leaves you feeling overwhelmed. You can reduce your stress levels by saying no to things that will increase your load unnecessarily, and by being selective of what you take on.

Stretch and Drink Lots of Water

When we are under a lot of stress, we often tense up, resulting in our muscles to contract and develop tension. We might also miss out on drinking enough water. Water is essential for the proper functioning of our body and for reducing our stress levels.

Stress has a more serious effect on two areas of the body: our hips, shoulders, and traps. Our shoulders and traps carry some of our most serious stress. The stress is most commonly a result of worrying about the future, about something that hasn't happened or something that might occur in the future. Most of the time, it's related to something that's lingering or building over time. It can cause fatigue, poor posture, and headaches. Moreover, the way we sleep, carry our bags, or look at our phones can also cause tension in our shoulders and traps, and this adds stress to our overall body.

Doing side-to-side neck stretches and head circles slowly can help combat stress in your shoulders and traps. Remember to pull your shoulders back while doing these stretches. You also need to have a good posture while stretching. Massaging is also an effective way to relieve pain, decrease the buildup of lactic acid (soreness), and reduce stress. You can also apply an ice pack and a heating pack alternatively to help relax your neck and shoulder muscles.

Our hips also carry a lot of stress, although we might not realize it. They work so hard, both directly and indirectly. They can become tight because of standing or sitting for too long. Mental stress can also accumulate in the hips. Moreover, tight hips can also minimize your performance and result in back pain.

Stretching every day for ten or fifteen minutes can help combat stress in the hips. Pay special attention to your hamstrings, quads, and flexors to release the tension in your hips. You can also use a foam roller on your glutes and hip flexors. These actions can help relieve any built-up tension present in your hips. Lastly, another effective tension-releasing strategy is to lie flat on your back with your legs up against the wall. This can cause some relief in your hips and legs by allowing the gravity to pull the blood back to your hips.

Even though these techniques sound so simple, we often miss out on these. A simple stretch at your desk or a reminder to get those water moments can make a world of difference.

Get Some Quality Sleep

Stress can make you lose sleep. However, a lack of sleep is also a major cause of stress. Your body and brain can get out of whack due to this vicious cycle, and it only gets worse with time.

Getting the recommended 7 to 8 hours of sleep can have an enormous impact on your life and quality of life. Try to dim the lights, turn off the TV earlier, and give yourself some time to relax before going to sleep. Getting some quality sleep might be the most effective stress buster for most of us.

Try a Body Scan

Try to scan your body mentally to get a sense of how it gets affected by stress every day. You can sit with your feet on the floor or lie on your back. Take three deep breaths and scan your body from head to toe without any judgment. How does your forehead feel? Are you relaxed or scrunched? How does your mouth feel? Tight or loose? Start at your toes and keep moving up, simply noticing how every section of your body feels.

Exercise

Exercising is one of the best things you can do to relieve stress. Although it might seem contradictory, mental stress can be relieved by exerting physical stress on your body by exercising. Exercising regularly can provide the best benefits.

Studies show that people who exercise daily are less likely to have anxiety or stress-related problems than those who don't exercise. Some of the reasons behind this are:

- **Confidence** – Exercising can make you feel more confident and competent with your body. This can, in turn, promote your mental well-being.
- **Sleep** – Stress and anxiety can negatively impact your sleep quality. Exercising can improve the quality of your sleep.
- **Stress hormone** – In the long run, exercising regularly can lower the secretion of stress hormones like cortisol. It can also improve your mood by releasing endorphins, which are like chemicals that act like natural painkillers.

You can do any exercise routine or activity that you enjoy, like yoga, rock climbing, dancing, or walking. Activities that involve repetitive movements of large muscle groups – like walking or jogging – can be stress-relieving.

Practice Mindfulness

Practicing mindfulness can help anchor you to the present moment. It can help fight the stress-inducing effects of negative thinking. There are various ways of increasing mindfulness, such as meditation, yoga, mindfulness-based stress reduction, and mindfulness-based cognitive therapy. A recent study conducted on college students also found that mindful approaches can help improve self-esteem, which can, in turn, decrease the symptoms of depression and anxiety (Lindsay Maxwell, 2016).

The process of meditation involves quieting your mind through breathing techniques. Studies have proven that meditation has several mental health benefits along with its ability to rewire the brain. A study published in *Psychiatry Research* has revealed that meditating for a minimum of two minutes every day can help you harness its benefits, which include permanently rewiring your brain.

Try Yoga

Yoga has gained popularity as a way of stress relief and exercise among all age groups. Even though the styles of yoga may differ, the majority share the same goal – to connect your mind and body. This happens by enhancing your body and breath awareness.

Studies have revealed that yoga can improve your mood and might even be as effective at treating anxiety and depression as anti-depressant drugs. The benefits of yoga in relieving stress and anxiety are mainly related to its effects on your stress response and nervous system. It can also decrease your heart rate, blood pressure, and cortisol levels as well as increase the levels of the neurotransmitter GABA (gamma-aminobutyric acid), which is reduced in mood disorders.

Reduce Your Caffeine Intake

Caffeine is a stimulant present in energy drinks, chocolates, tea, and coffee. When consumed in high doses can increase anxiety.

Different people have different thresholds for the amount of caffeine they are able to tolerate. Consider cutting back on your caffeine consumption if you notice that it's making you anxious or jittery. Even though several studies show that when consumed in moderate amounts, it can be healthy, it is not for everyone. In general, five or lesser cups each day is considered a reasonable amount.

Spend Time With Your Family and Friends

In stressful times, social support from your family and friends can help you a lot. Having a network of friends can provide you with a sense of self-worth and belonging, which can help you in stressful situations.

Research has revealed that for women, in particular, oxytocin (which is a natural stress reliever) gets released when they spend time with their friends and children. This effect is known as 'tend and befriend,' which is the opposite of the fight or flight response (Shelley E. Taylor, 2000).

Remember that both men, as well as women, benefit from friendship. Another research revealed that men and women who had less social connections had a higher chance of suffering from anxiety and depression (Renee B. Cadzow, 2009).

Learn to Avoid Procrastination

Staying on top of your priorities and avoiding procrastination is another method of taking control of your stress levels. Procrastination can leave you scrambling to catch up by making you act reactively. This reactivity can result in stress, which can negatively influence the quality of your sleep as well as your health.

To prevent procrastination, you can make it a habit to construct a do-to list organized by your priorities. Try giving yourself realistic deadlines and make your way down the list. Give yourself lots of uninterrupted time and work on the tasks that need to be done immediately. Multitasking or switching between tasks can also be stressful in itself.

Listen to Soothing Music

Listening to the music you like can have a very relaxing and soothing effect on your body and is a positive way of relieving stress. Slow-paced instrumental music can start the relaxation response by reducing your heart rate, blood pressure, as well as stress hormones. Just listening to the kind of music you like can be effective in reducing stress. The sounds of nature can also be very calming, and that's why they are often used in making meditation and relaxation music.

Eat Right

Stress levels are closely related to a proper diet. We often forget to eat well when we are overwhelmed and end up going to fatty, sugary foods as a pick-me-up. Plan ahead and try to avoid sugary foods. Fish with high amounts of omega-3-fatty acids, fruits, and vegetables have been proven to decrease stress symptoms.

Be Grateful

Try to keep at least a few gratitude journals. You can keep one at work, one in your purse, and one at home by your bed. If that feels like too much, even just recording a short message on your phone can help bring these moments to light. They could help you remember all the things that are going well in your life. Try to be grateful for your blessings in life. Being grateful can help cancel out your negative thoughts and worries.

Using these journals will help you savor all your good experiences, such as good health, a sunshine-filled day, or even a child's smile. Remember to celebrate even small accomplishments like mastering a new hobby or a new task at work. Spend some time looking through your notes whenever you start to feel stressed and remind yourself of the things that matter.

Call to Action:

At the end of the day, try to recount three moments that made you laugh. Continue this for seven days. It could be a chuckle, a giggle, or full-on roaring laughter. Either way, write it down. Re-read these moments after seven days and see how you feel. Could you keep this going?

7

CONNECTING WITH YOUR BODY

A re you searching for an easy way to enhance the quality of your life? Well, you don't need to search much further than your own body and mind. Research reveals that your health and well-being is significantly affected by your attitudes, feelings, and thoughts. This belief is, however, not a new, trendy fad. Mind-body techniques are being used in various settings as an extra tool in the treatment of physical and psychological diseases. Studies have revealed that incorporating these practices as a part of personal training regimes as well as in professional clinical settings has shown to have promising positive outcomes. Staying connected with our bodies can impact our health and day to day living. Such things as high blood pressure, heart disease, depression, and overall mood can all be improved with the mind-body connection.

The connection between mind and body can be strengthened through several health approaches such as visualization, yoga, meditation, and qigong. You may not know much about qigong, but it is rooted in a history that dates back to more than three thousand years.

QIGONG AS A MIND-BODY CONNECTION PRACTICE

Qigong, pronounced as chee gong, is an ancient Chinese practice that incorporates meditation, gentle movements, and breathwork. The vital energy or life force is known as qi, while gong suggests working with qi. Combined, the practice of qigong is a beautifully blended exercise of utilizing, balancing, cultivating, and strengthening your energy with meditation, mindfulness, visualization, breath, and movement.

Qigong is a gentle, inexpensive, non-strenuous, and convenient way of bringing in mindful moments that help you live a healthier life and connect your body with your mind. This connection and gentle approach is what makes this practice so appealing. You can try working on your qi when you feel stressed, stiff, or emotionally down. There are several types of qigong and numerous methods to begin your own practice. Experimenting and finding a unique routine can help boost both your physical and mental well-being.

Qigong exercises are designed to help you enlighten your Shen, balance the flow of qi energy, and preserve your Jing. The dynamic meditations and exercises have Yin and Yang aspects: while Yin suggests *being it*, Yang means *doing it*. The Yin exercises of qigong are expressed in a more dynamic or aerobic method. The spiritual and physical exercises help move the qi energy through the 12 primary channels and eight added channels, strengthening it, smoothing the flow, and balancing it. In China, qigong is extensively used for people who have cancer. As it is a powerful tool for managing and restoring harmony, these exercises help extend longevity, prevent illness, and maintain health.

Anyone of any physical condition or age can practice qigong. You don't need to bench press a car or run a marathon in order to pursue healthfulness and reap the benefits. You can pick whatever suits your personal constitution when you design your qigong meditation or exercise practice.

THE BASIC TECHNIQUES OF QIGONG EXERCISE

Concentration

Concentration results from qigong exercises, breathing techniques, and qi energy awareness, show that it involves focusing on and letting go at the same moment. However, focusing does not suggest that you have to strain and wrinkle your forehead to pay attention. Instead, you will be able to construct a frame of mind that is big enough to encompass your whole body, mind, and spirit's functions by expanding your consciousness and deep relaxation. You'll be focused enough to allow the everyday hassles, worries, and distractions to drift away. The Ying/Yang concept is epitomized by this inward focus that expands outwards and helps you merge with the rhythms of the universe. While Yang energy tends to be more concentrated, Ying energy is more expansive. Depending on the situation, some people require more or less Yin or Yang. You will realize that as you continue practicing qigong meditation and exercises, you will become more proficient at this type of concentration, as it is the innate expression of qigong. You will realize that you have a higher power to affect your qi energy as you learn to concentrate more effectively.

Breathing

Lao Tzu, in the 6th century BCE, was the first to describe breathing techniques as a method to stimulate qi energy. 2 kinds of breathing exercises evolved from there: Daoist's Breath and Buddha's breath. Both methods help focus on meditation by infusing the body with qi.

- **Buddha's Breathe –** Extend your stomach while

inhaling to fill it up with air. Contract your stomach while exhaling and expel all the air out from the bottom of your lungs and then push it up and out until your chest and stomach get deflated. You can practice inhaling for a slow count of 8 and exhaling for a slow count of 16. Imagine you're inviting your qi energy to pass through the channels as you breathe in and out. Invite your qi to flow by using your mind. You have to guide the flow and not push or tug at it.

- **Daoist's Breath –** This pattern is the opposite of Buddha's breath. Contract your abdominal muscles when you breathe in and relax your lungs and torso while exhaling.

Remember that qigong is a technique of building awareness as you move through these steps. However, you feel comfortable following the routine is what's right for you at that moment.

BENEFITS OF PRACTICING QIGONG

Qigong has been shown to have several psychological as well as physical benefits. Some of the most notable benefits of practicing qigong are:

Improvement of Mental Health

Practices like qigong that involve mindfulness-based techniques can be beneficial for those who suffer from mental health issues. It has shown to improve several areas of mental health, including reduced stress, cognitive function, and emotional regulation. A 2008 study found a decrease in PTSD symptoms in individuals who suffered from extreme psychological and physical trauma (Michael A. Grodin, 2008).

A systematic review conducted in 2013 concluded that the psychological benefits of qigong included improved mood and reduced depressive symptoms (Fang Wang, 2013). Overall, it showed a positive impact on the quality of life, anxiety, depression, and stress management. Another study published in 2019 showed that COPD (chronic obstructive pulmonary disease) patients who practiced qigong for at least thirty minutes 3 times every week had an effective reduction in depression (Zaimin Li, 2019). The patients who practiced this exercise for thirty to sixty minutes were found to have an improvement in their anxiety symptoms. The duration (twenty-four weeks in this study) played an important role in increasing the effectiveness of decreasing anxiety.

Nurturing the Heart and Lungs

People suffering from COPD often experience difficulty in breathing and tend to feel limited in their ability to exercise.

Studies have shown that qigong can improve the quality of life by enhancing their ability to exercise, their mental health, and pulmonary function.

Hypertension or high blood pressure is a common condition that can increase an individual's risk of heart diseases. A systematic literature review conducted in 2015 showed that qigong accompanied by anti-hypersensitive medications can significantly decrease systolic as well as diastolic blood pressure as compared to when drugs are used alone (Xingjiang Xiong, 2015). Moreover, it was found that in patients who were not using any other methods to manage their blood pressure, qigong had a profound effect on reducing their blood pressure measurements.

Relief for Muscle, Tissue, and Joint Pain

Chronic pain can be very weakening. The term arthritis is used to describe the different kinds of joint diseases. These joint diseases can result in chronic pain accompanied by swelling and stiffness in the joints and other connective tissues. Fatigue, depression, limited function, and mobility can have an adverse effect on a person's well-being. A comprehensive study conducted in 2017 concluded that qigong was effective in improving mental health and decreasing pain and might help improve the quality of life of people who have arthritis (Ray Marks, 2017).

Similarly, another painful condition known as fibromyalgia can also cause digestive issues, sensitivities, headaches, fatigue, sleep disturbances, and more. Even though it's still not confirmed how effective qigong can be for individuals who have fibromyalgia, it might serve as a complementary tool for providing relief from fatigue, pain, and depression.

A study published in the International Journal of Environmental Research and Public Health in the year 2018 studied the data from over twenty-five studies (Liye Zou, 2018). They concluded that qigong might also be a useful practice for individuals who experience widespread body pain, lower back pain, knee pain, shoulder pain, and neck pain. A person's sleep quality can also be affected by chronic pain. Qigong can help improve the quality of sleep in patients suffering from chronic conditions such as hypertension, diabetes, insomnia, and in conditions that affected the nerves, tendons, bones, and muscles.

VIPASSANA

Vipassana is another simple method of finding that mind-body connection. It is a simple, convenient, and practical way of achieving real peace of mind to lead a happy and useful life. It is one of India's most ancient methods of meditation. It was rediscovered by Gautama Buddha by almost twenty-five hundred years ago and is the essence of what he taught and practiced in this 45-year ministry. Buddhism addresses two main kinds of meditation techniques. They differ in the qualities of consciousness, modes of function, and mental skills. They are called Vipassana and Samatha in Pali. While Vipassana can be translated as 'Insight,' Samatha translated to 'tranquility' or 'concentration.'

Vipassana is a gentle yet very thorough technique. It is an ancient and codified mode of training your mind. It requires a set of exercises that helps you to become more and more aware of your own life experiences. It involves careful testing, mindful seeing, and attentive listening. You can learn to touch fully, smell accurately, and ultimately pay attention to the changes that are happening in all these experiences. It helps you to listen to your own thoughts without getting caught up in them. The Vipassana meditation technique aims to help you learn to see the art of selflessness, satisfactoriness, and the truth of impermanence. We might think that we're already doing this. However, that's an illusion. It occurs because we pay so little attention to the continual surge of our own life experiences that we might just be sleeping. We simply do not pay enough attention to understand that we are not paying attention.

Vipassana is a kind of mental training that aims to teach you to experience the world in a completely new way. It is a method of self-discovery, a participatory investigation through which you can observe your own life experiences while taking part in them while they occur. I have not tried this personally, however, if you are up for ten days of silence and no talking, I know someone who went through this. It is an intense (intense in that there is no talking or writing allowed) way to get in touch with your body and your mind. There are no medications, no books, no meat allowed. You are housed and fed. You have daily, timed sessions with a counselor. Outside of this, there are no phones or communication. It is literally an electronics and vocal detox. Can we even fathom a moment where our world is silent for longer than 30 minutes? We sleep, and then we are inundated with electronics, the news, our children (sweet things that they are!), our phones, our computers, our choices, our day, our calendar, our meetings, and everything in between. I can only imagine being silent for ten days would take us to a place where we have never been before. I realize that most of us cannot take ten days to be silent; however, it's meant to spur on the idea that even 2 minutes might be helpful. Can we spare 2 minutes of the 1,440 minutes in a day?

THE PRACTICE OF VIPASSANA

Practicing Vipassana meditation involves following the principles of the universal law of nature or Dharma. It includes following the noble eightfold path, which is broadly classified into Panna (insight, wisdom), Samadhi (concentration), and Sila (Mortality). It is necessary to undertake a 10-day residential course under the counsel of a qualified teacher to learn Vipassana. The classes are conducted at Vipassana Centers and several non-center places as well. Students remain inside the course site throughout the entire duration of the retreat. They have no contact with the outside world. They are required to suspend all disciplines and religious practices and refrain from reading and writing as well. The participants also have to follow a prescribed Code of Disciple during the entire course. They also maintain noble silence by not talking with a fellow participant. However, they can discuss material problems with the management and meditation questions with the teacher. Students are also welcome to leave at any time, as this is a voluntary stay.

The training has three main steps:

First, the participants practice sila (mortality) by abstaining from actions that can cause harm. It takes on five moral principles, practicing abstention from the use of intoxicants, lying, sexual misconduct, stealing, and killing. Even to the degree that if they see a bug in a room, they are not allowed to kill it, Instead, they can take it back outside to live where it is meant to live. The observation of these principles helps the mind calm down sufficiently so that it can proceed with the task at hand.

The **second** step is to practice Anapana for the 1st three and a half days by focusing attention on breathing. This practice can help gain control over the unruly mind and develop Samadhi (concentration). The 1sttwo steps of developing control over the mind and living a wholesome life are essential and extremely beneficial. However, they are incomplete without undertaking the 3rd step, which involves cleansing the mind of underlying mental impurities.

In the **3rd** step, which lasts for six and a half days, one gains the clarity of panna (wisdom, insight) by the practice of Vipassana. One can penetrate one's entire mental and physical structure during this step.

The participants receive systematic instructions many times every day, and the progress of the day is described during a taped discourse at the end of the day. The students maintain complete silence for the first nine days. They resume speaking on the 10th day to make the transition back to a more extroverted way of everyday life. The retreat ends on the morning of the 11th day. It concludes with the practice of metta-bhavana, which is a technique of meditation in which the purity obtained during the retreat is shared with everyone else.

BENEFITS OF VIPASSANA

Some of the major benefits of Vipassana are:

- **Increased awareness** – Change is not possible if you don't gain awareness. At Vipassana retreats, you have wake up at 4 a.m. and go to sleep at 10 p.m. These long days give you lots of time for self-reflection. You gain awareness about all the positive and negative aspects of your personality as well as life. Setting some time aside every day gives you a chance to attain this reflection. You can feel more attuned to your emotions with the help of this improved awareness.

- **Remaining equanimous** – Being equanimous, no matter what you experience, is the primary teaching of Vipassana meditation. Equanimity involves accepting all outcomes, whether it's good or bad. So, you don't get attached or cling on to a pleasant, enjoyable experience. Similarly, you don't avert bad experiences. Remain equanimous and accept everything as it is.

- **Impermanence** – Everything you know, including yourself, the people in your life as well as all your possessions will eventually grow old and die. You are constantly reminded of this during the ten days of retreat. Understanding that your life is in a constant flux helps you to accept the things in your life just as they are. This realization can also help make hard periods a little bit easier.

- **Detox from life** – You observe noble silence for ten days. You are not allowed any writing or reading material or electronic devices. As we spend our typical lives in a constant state of stimulation, it might seem strange and challenging practice. Eliminating all these distractions help keep you concentrated on practicing meditation. As you are not taking in any new information, it helps decrease the pace of your thoughts. This lack of additional stimulus enables a much better detox and a more in-depth focus on meditation.

- **Learning to fail** – The aim of meditation is to focus on your breath and thereby concentrate on your mind. This helps calm your mind. However, unless you reach enlightenment, you can never stay entirely without thoughts. The state of enlightenment is still impermanent. You can build your perseverance and willpower by practicing daily throughout these failures. It helps make you comfortable with failure, and this bleeds into the different parts of your life.

- **Broader perspective** – The practice of

Vipassana can provide you with a broader perspective on situations. You start to understand that all the problems that are affecting you are a manifestation of your thoughts rather than looking outward. You begin to take responsibility for your own life.

- **Improved mobility** – It could be painful to sit cross-legged for ten hours a day. For a majority of you, the first few days will be painful. However, as your body gets used to it sitting, your hips start to open. Sitting cross-legged with your knees and tail bone touching the ground, and your spine straight puts you in a perfect position to sit comfortably for longer periods of time.

- **Improved efficiency with time** – Through the Vipassana retreat, you can learn to slow down and listen. If your mind is always crammed with thoughts about what you 'should' be doing, this experience can. Try to focus on two-three important tasks and forget about everything else. You can have a greater concentration while carrying out tasks by being more present. All of this leads to completing tasks quicker with more efficiency. Again, you may not be able to take ten days off to go to a retreat; however, look at this in a much broader sense and see the benefits of meditation and mindful choices.

Again, this method of meditation and this retreat may not be right for you, and that's okay! I'm giving such an extensive look into this form of meditation because there is value in this retreat. Whether you do this or not, the value within meditation is boundless.

HOW CAN FOOD AFFECT THE WAY YOU FEEL?

Our brain is always 'on' and works hard throughout the day and night, even when we are asleep. It takes care of our senses, heartbeat, breathing, as well as our movements. This is why the brain needs a constant supply of fuel. This fuel is obtained from the foods we eat, and the contents of the fuel make all the difference. Simply put, the foods we eat directly affect the function and structure of our brain as well as our mood. Consuming high-quality foods that have a lot of antioxidants, minerals, and vitamins provide nourishment to the brain and protects it from oxidative stress. The free radicals produced as waste when the body utilizes oxygen can damage cells.

Unfortunately, when we consume foods like processed or refined foods, or foods high in refined sugar, it can be harmful to the brain. In addition to increasing oxidative stress and inflammation, they can also affect our body's regulation of insulin. Several studies have found a connection between a diet rich in refined sugars and impaired brain function as well as a worsening of symptoms of mood disorders, including depression. Even though mindful eating doesn't necessarily require a change in what you eat, taking steps to eat nutritious foods will have an enormous impact on your health in the future.

Even though the medical field does not fully acknowledge the connection between food and mood, the burgeoning field of nutritional psychiatry is now starting to recognize that there are several correlations and consequences between not only the food you eat and how you feel and behave but also the types of bacteria living in our guts. We touched on this a bit in chapter 2; however, let's take another look at this now.

The neurotransmitter serotonin helps inhibit pain, mediate moods, and regulate appetite and sleep. The inner workings of our digestive system not only help us digest food, but they also guide our emotions. This is because almost ninety-five percent of our serotonin is released in the gastrointestinal tract. The tract is lined with millions of neurons or nerve cells. Moreover, the production of serotonin and the functions of these neurons are highly influenced by the several millions of good bacteria that constitute your intestinal microbiome. These bacteria have an important role in your health. They protect the intestinal lining and provide a strong barrier against bad bacteria and harmful toxins. They also activate the neural pathway that connects the gut and the brain and also improves our absorption of nutrients from food.

Researchers have made comparisons between 'traditional' diets, like the traditional Japanese diet and the Mediterranean diet, to a typical 'Western' diet. They found that the risk of depression is twenty-five percent to thirty-five percent less in those who eat a traditional diet. They accounted for this difference because the traditional diets contain a modest quantity of dairy and lean meats, and tend to be higher in seafood, fish, unprocessed grains, fruits, and vegetables. They also don't have sugars and processed and refined foods, which form the staples of the 'Western' diet. Moreover, a majority of these unprocessed foods are fermented and thus act as natural probiotics.

So, what does nutritional psychiatry mean for you? You can start by paying attention to how consuming different foods make you feel – not only in the present moment but also the following day. You can try having a 'clean' diet devoid of all sugars and processed foods for 2 to 3 weeks. Think about how hard our bodies work from minute to minute. Take a moment to appreciate all the ways that it helps us live our day to day lives. Think about the fuel that it needs to keep going. What you eat affects the way our bodies move through the day.

Call to Action:

Once you have worked through the last call to action, take 2 minutes to sit in silence for the next seven days. Eyes closed, guided with an app that can take you through a meditation. You could do this with an app called Calm or Headspace, or simply head over to Youtube and do a search for a guided meditation. Carve out 2 minutes, or more, for silence. Acknowledge the thoughts in your mind, and tell them to float on by. You can always come back to them.

8

WHAT MATTERS MOST – TASTE, FUNCTION, OR NUTRITION?

Confucius had said that very few people could appreciate taste even though everyone eats and drinks. We can join those few who appreciate it when we understand a little about the science of taste. The science of taste is, in fact, amazing. The human sensory systems allow us to differentiate between more than 100,000 different types of flavors. Flavors emerge from the ability of our body to distinguish one taste from another. I can't stand chicken—the smell of it, the feel of it. Give me a chicken with a creamy sauce, some asparagus, and sun-dried tomatoes on top, and I'm set though! It's all in how the chicken is prepared! I have realized over time that my taste-buds prefer savory and salty in healthy foods. My taste buds also prefer sweet and creamy in desserts.

Why is it that some people love raw veggies, but hate them

cooked? Or some people can't even deal with the taste of broccoli at all? Why do we vary so much with spicy foods or even sweet treats? Why do some of us seek out tangy and spicy meals at a restaurant while others stick with the familiar? How often during a meal do we take the time to discover why we enjoy what we enjoy or why we choose what we choose. Recent studies are showing that the connection between our taste buds and our nervous system is showing that this matters, not only for taste but also for our health.

Our sense of smell and taste is definitely linked to our overall health status. Several studies have revealed that the flavor of the food we're eating is one of the most critical factors that determine the kind of food we choose to eat. The flavor of the food isn't something we can sense, however, it is created in our brain based on what we smell with the help of our nose and taste with the help of our mouth. Flavor, smell, and taste are distinctly separate from each other. Learning to recognize smells comes from experience, whereas the sense of taste can be seen in newborn infants within the age of 6 months as it is built into our genes.

THE DIFFERENCE BETWEEN TASTE AND FLAVOR

You might not realize what you are eating if you close your eyes and hold your nose while eating a chocolate bar. Chocolate might just taste sweet or bitter to you without your sense of smell. It's not only our taste buds that affect things, but it's also our sense of smell. Think about having a head cold. How well can you taste when you have a head cold?

The flavor is much more than just taste and odor. It also includes temperature and texture, as well as a sense of pain. Combine it all, and you get the ability to distinguish between more than 100,000 different flavors.

What Are the Basic Taste Sensations?

Reports in the US National Library of Medicine, the world's most extensive medical library, identified five particular kinds of taste. Our brain receives these taste sensations from the taste receptors present in our mouth. The five sensations are:

- **Savory** – This taste comes from the amino acids (protein building blocks) present naturally in foods rich in protein like cheese and meats.
- **Sour** – This is the taste of acidic products such as organic acids and lemon juice.

- **Bitter –** This is the taste of thirty-five different proteins present in plants.
- **Salty –** This is the taste of salt crystals (sodium and chloride) and the mineral salts magnesium and potassium.
- **Sweet –** This is the taste of the natural sugars present in honey, as well as several fruits.

Scientists are actively searching for new taste receptors. There is a growing acceptance of fat as the 6th taste sensation. Taste receptors for water, calcium, starch, metallic, alkaline (opposite of sour), and fat might also be added in the future.

How Did Our Sense of Smell and Taste Evolve?

When we sit down to eat our favorite food, we often take it for granted that we'll taste and savor the various flavors present in our meal. We seldom think about our sense of taste because it has become so central to our daily lives. However, researchers are discovering that the sense of taste is anything but ordinary. It is a very complex neurobiological process that is affected by several factors like experience, age, and genes.

Researchers believe that our sense of taste evolved to protect us from consuming food items that might be poisonous and to make sure that we get all the nutrients and calories that we require. Several kinds of poisons are either sour or bitter – tastes that we often reject. On the other hand, our enjoyment of sweet and salty food items ensures that we meet our nutritional requirements for carbohydrates (including sugars) and salts (particularly sodium chloride). A 5th taste receptor, umami (which is Japanese for 'savory'), encourages us to consume food items rich in amino acid glutamate, which is present in tomatoes, cheese, and meats.

Our ability to sense all of these tastes is thought to have evolved to increase our earliest ancestor's chances of survival. Salt is needed for regulating our fluid levels in our bodies. Umami is known to have developed as a means to identify essential amino acids and proteins. The sweet taste of fruits reveals a source of sugars required for energy. Sour helps point out the presence of spoiled foods, which we might find in old milk. Fat is another necessary source of essential amino acids, as well as energy. Our sense of taste evolved to help us identify non-volatile molecules that we might not be able to smell.

However, what gives some of us a high sensitivity and others low sensitivity to some tastes? Neuroscientists are now studying the receptor cells and their genetic influences to answer this as well as other questions about the sensation of taste. Such studies have led to:

- Effective strategies for helping individuals avoid overeating and gaining weight.
- Identification of factors that affect taste preferences.
- Insight into how the brain manages sensory stimuli.

On the other hand, humans are able to identify more than 10,000 different kinds of odor compared to the fewer number of basic tastes. Unlike taste, we are very sensitive to smell. We can identify the aroma of particular volatile substances at the level of one part per trillion, and some even at levels a thousand times lower. In simpler terms, one part per trillion is the same as 1 second in 32,000 years.

Our amazing sense of smell is thought to have evolved to help us locate food and avoid eating spoiled food items without tasting them. You might have seen your sensitivity to smell in case of a natural gas leak. To help us detect even small leaks, gas companies add traces of methyl mercaptan, which is a very smelly volatile sulfur-containing compound to the natural gas. We can detect this compound at two parts per billion. Even though it is a small amount, it is still about a thousand times more concentrated than 1 part per trillion. We can smell some compounds like roasted oats, molds, green bell pepper, etc. at levels of a part per trillion and even lower.

HOW DO TASTE AND SMELL REACH OUR BRAIN?

We can sense the smell of food by two different routes. Retronasal smell is the aroma that is released into our nose through the back of our mouth when we chew and swallow food. In contrast, orthonasal smell is the aroma we get by sniffing through our nose. Retronasal and orthonasal smells seem to be processed in separate regions of the brain. Retronasal smell is considered the most important route for sensing the smell of food and is believed to make up about eighty to eighty-five percent of the flavor of food. This explains why we are not able to detect the flavor of our food when our nose is blocked due to a cold. Special receptor proteins present on the surface of the olfactory and taste cells in our nose and mouth help sense the aroma and taste of food. These cells provide a direct connection between our brain and the outside world.

Taste starts in the mouth, where all of us have about five thousand to ten thousand taste buds. The majority of the taste buds are situated within the papillae, which are the visible bumps present on the tongue. However, some taste buds can also present in other regions of the mouth and throat. About fifty to a hundred taste receptor cells are present on each taste bud. These are neurons or brain cells that transmit information about food. For instance, when we eat a strawberry, the chemicals present in the fruit are dissolved by the saliva, which then binds to the taste cells by entering into the central pores of the taste buds. These taste cells then quickly transmit 'sweet' and 'sour' signals to the brain through the nerve fibers. They finally reach the sensory cortex in the brain. The flavor of the strawberry, however, also requires the extra information through the sense of smell.

ROLE OF TASTE PREFERENCES IN AFFECTING CHOICE AND CONSUMPTION OF FOODS

Repeated consumption of high-energy but nutrient-poor foods can result in undesirable health conditions like obesity. Taste has a vital role in our choice of foods. A better understanding of the connections between our food choices, individual taste preferences, and taste of foods can help us understand why some people choose to eat unhealthy foods.

A variety of different studies reveal that one of the most important drivers of food consumption is actually food liking. It includes enjoyment of the six primary taste sensations – fat, umami, salty, bitter, and sour. A group of researchers conducted a study focusing on how taste likely can influence the choice and consumption of both nutrient-rich and nutrient-poor foods (Djin Gie Liem, 2019).

Foods rich in energy but poor in nutrients dominate today's modern industrialized food supply. These foods are readily available due to ease of consumption, low prices, and high volumes. However, they are highly processed and rich in sodium, saturated fat, and sugars. An increase in the accessibility of such foods is associated with an increase in consumption. The taste profile of food can be significantly impacted by sodium, fat, and sugar. Mapping this against the nutrient-rich food (NFR) index, they hypothesized that individual nutrient-rich and nutrient-poor foods have different taste profiles. Similarly, they also hypothesized that the taste profiles of healthy diets that predominantly consist of nutrient-rich foods are different than unhealthy diets, which are dominated by unhealthy foods.

Modern advances in how we produce our food have made it harder and harder to believe our taste buds and determine whether a food is nutritious. For example, bread can seem less salty than chips at the same sodium content. This is because, compared to the sodium on the surface of the chips, the sodium present in bread is less accessible to the sodium sensing channels present on our tongue. Moreover, modern advancements have also been able to decouple some nutrient composition and sensory profiles. For instance, non-nutrient sweeteners can add a sweet taste to foods without added calories. Thus, the content of nutrients in food might not match the perceived taste intensity.

Why do we reach for Hershey's milk chocolate over a bar of dark chocolate with70% cocoa content? Could we be sensitive to the bitterness of this dark chocolate because we have been ingesting processed stuff for too long? The more chocolate is processed, the more it loses the qualities that make it healthy in the first place. The point is, try to stick to whole food and less processed foods. Bear in mind that none of this is to say that you can't have milk chocolate!! It's all about bringing those mindful moments into the picture with variety, recognizing how taste affects our health, and working towards a whole foods way of living, with everything else scattered into the mix.

Call to Action:

Take a moment to have a snack. Choose a few things. Maybe a bit of chocolate, some strawberries, and some cheese. Yum!! Plug your nose and take a bite of something. How does it feel in your mouth, what do you notice not being able to smell the food? After you have done this with all three. Next, take a bite and leave your nose unplugged. Take in the smell and taste of the food. How do these impact things?

9

MINDFUL EATING SOCIAL STRATEGIES

Pursuing mindful eating can sometimes seem unrealistic, especially in social events. Social events and consumption are often connected, and they can bring up stress and anxiety. We touched on this a bit in a previous chapter. However, let's dig even deeper now. Some people try to avoid them, fearing that they might end up overeating or go off a particular diet. When we are focused on others, it's easy to go into mindless eating and end up feeling overfull. It is important to keep these social moments and spontaneity in play. Don't fear these moments, but create some space to make them what you genuinely want them to be. These are moments to enjoy. Be a part of the lives of people you care about and want to be within that moment. If you're only present with how your body is feeling with what you're eating, you won't be able to be present with your company. This is not ideal for your health as well. You can learn how to maximize the nourishment that social events can offer with the help of a few reminders and guidelines. They can help prevent anxiety, pre-event fear, or post-event stomach upset or bloat.

On the weekends, eating with others can be one of the hardest moments when it comes to practicing mindful eating. It becomes easy to get swept away when you are with friends and family, and you can then become unaware of what you ingest in a social moment. It is good to be able to recognize that weekends might require completely different mindful moments than weekdays. Weekdays are often some-what scheduled or routined, but the weekends can be spon-taneous and unplanned. Leaving room for more moments of mindfulness is important and can help you learn how to plan ahead, stay mindful, and enjoy the food as well as the company.

HOW DO SOCIAL GATHERINGS CHALLENGE MINDFUL EATING?

From sugary punch bowls to enticing dessert tables, social gatherings are infamous for putting mindfulness techniques to the test. This is because we tend to eat more in the pres-ence of other people. Psychology explains this phenomenon as the 'social facilitation of eating.' This term is used by experts to describe how the presence of other people can influence our eating behaviors.

An article published in *Physiology & Behavior* in 2017 explains that we tend to eat more when we are with company as it enables social bonding. The act of talking while eating, particularly helps to create a positive atmosphere. These experiences generally evoke relaxation and joy, which fuels our tendency to continue eating. It is all because of the 'feel-good' hormone endorphin. These hormones are typically associated with a runner's high.

An article published in *Adaptive Human Behavior and Physiology* in the year 2017 suggests that much like dancing and laughing, eating also activates our endorphin systems. This secretion of endorphins encourages a sense of closeness with those we are experiencing the activity with, and this leads to the release of even more endorphins. This release simply means that we end up eating more at social gatherings because it makes our brains happy.

STRATEGIES TO PRACTICE MINDFUL EATING AT SOCIAL GATHERINGS

Practicing mindful eating when you are at social events might feel like an added task. However, following these simple strategies, you can allow yourself room for presence and awareness to flourish naturally while still enjoying the event.

Similar to any other lifestyle practices, it is best to adopt these strategies, aiming for small changes gradually. They can become second nature for mindful eating over time and develop into your plus one at all events.

Here are some strategies to put into play when being a part of social moments:

Eat Before You Leave

Taking charge before you even arrive is one of the easiest ways to manage your appetite at a social event. You might think that you're going to an event where you can eat a lot and don't need to eat until you reach it. However, when you reach the event with this mindset and an empty stomach, you give yourself the opportunity for ravenous eating.

It is recommended that you eat a snack packed with fibers and protein before leaving the house, to offset this temptation. As these nutrients are very filling, they will make you feel satiated for extended periods of time. You can also consider some plantain chips with guacamole, string cheese with grapes, or a handful of almonds.

However, in some moments, this may not be possible (such as a happy hour after work or some unplanned moment). If you can stop somewhere and pick up an apple or something else that might be light, it can help in filling you up a bit beforehand. Keeping yourself well-fed before going to a social event can help you avoid mindlessly grazing throughout the event.

Drink Water

Whether you're sweating in a spin class or lounging at your home, staying hydrated is very important. However, when you are at a social gathering, drinking water can change your eating habits throughout the event. According to the journal *Obesity*, drinking water helps reduce the intake of food by increasing the feeling of fullness. Moreover, dehydration can mask itself as hunger. So keep sipping on the water before as well as during the event. If you are hungry, you will still feel hungry after drinking water.

For a fair amount of people, eating at social events is also a habit born due to anxiety and nerves. Reaching for food and eating gives them something to do with their hands while they are talking to someone or standing alone between conversations. In such cases, grabbing a glass of water and drinking; it can serve as a stand-in for those tempting snacks you can't stop eating.

Therefore, it is recommended that you alternate between glasses of water and alcoholic beverages. This will help you stay mindful by slowing down a bit and will help you feel fuller, but you will also be able to prevent a possible hangover.

Eat Slowly

It can become very tempting to devour the hors d'oeuvres as fast as the champagne flows because of the high energy of social events. However, you can have more control over your eating habits if you eat slowly by taking the time to chew properly.

A study published in the journal *Cell Metabolism* revealed that satiety hormones such as peptide YY and glucagon-like peptide-1 are released by the gut when you eat food. These hormones send signals to your brain when it's time to stop eating by reducing your appetite. They also work to reduce the levels of the 'hunger hormone,' also known as ghrelin, as discussed in a previous chapter. However, the catch is that it takes approximately twenty minutes for these signals to reach your brain. By eating slowly, you can give your brain enough time to receive these hormonal signals.

Take long, mindful bites. You may be in conversation with other people, but this is still a chance to take those chews seriously. This will help you enjoy every bite, and help your brain stay in tune with your stomach and feel those fullness cues sooner. Try to truly savor the food by paying attention to its aroma, texture, and flavor.

Try to Mingle Away From Food

At social gatherings, the hosts often serve food buffet-style to allow the guests to fill up as they want. Even though the open format of buffet makes it easy to personalize your meal, it also makes it easy to graze as you converse with people mindlessly.

Therefore, I suggest that you simply walk away and invite the other person to sit somewhere else so that you can converse adequately as well as enjoy your food. You can avoid thoughtlessly refilling your plate while you converse by spending just a moment relocating yourself and your companion.

Eat In Small Doses

Some people tend to order a lot of food or load up their plates all at once. However, this means that you are likely to eat it all, even if you are already full because you're not paying attention to your eating. So, if it's possible, try to take only small servings. Then, even if you're not mindful at the moment, you won't end up doing much damage by consuming the entire serving.

Aim for Healthier Options

Even though you might be surrounded by a lot of rich, dense food, or junk foods at social events, there will also be some healthier options like salads, veggie sides, tea, or water instead of alcohol. It's not that you need to eat only healthy foods; however, it can be a great time to practice a mindful moment of choosing something healthier, then next time you can feel the freedom of choosing something that may feel a bit more indulgent.

Indulge Selectively

Even though it might seem counterintuitive, allowing yourself to enjoy your favorite foods can help keep your cravings in check.

A study published in *Frontiers of Psychology* in the year 2017, revealed that individuals who strictly avoid the foods that they crave end up developing a greater craving for that particular food. The study was conducted with thirty-nine participants who displayed a craving for chocolate, which was determined by a food questionnaire. The participants were not allowed to consume chocolate for two weeks. After several surveys, the researchers discovered that the 2-week deprivation of chocolates increased their cravings for chocolate. The researchers found that their reports supported the notion that flexible eating is more effective for managing food cravings as compared to strict dieting rules.

This report suggests that by allowing yourself to enjoy food in a reasonable way, you can put an end to the fixation while still treating yourself. If you stop eating particularly sweet food, it's more likely that you will eat more than you usually do or go home and binge eat because you feel deprived.

Have Cues

You can remind yourself to notice when you have finished eating a small serving and are about to get more even though you might not be able to pay close attention to your eating. Pause for a moment every time you are about to grab more food or drink and ask yourself why you are getting more food, are you hungry, or are you eating or drinking just because you need something to do while socializing. This way, each refill can turn into a mindfulness cue.

Stay Mindful While Engaging In Conversation

Eating in social situations daily is a fact of life for the majority of us. Following these strategies can help you stay attuned, enjoy your food, and be social at the same time.

- Practice being present in the conversation when you sit down to eat with others in social situations like celebrations, events, holidays, work, meetings, etc.
- Do you enjoy the foods on your plate, or might you

reach for something different? Just because it's on the table does not mean you have to partake. Enjoy the conversation at hand! Hold a drink in your hand to help keep your hands busy.

- Shift your attention to the experience of eating and how your body feels. Try to notice how hungry or satiated you might be and how good the food tastes. Allow your sensory experiences, your swallowing, and chewing to bring you fully back to eating. Be focused on that for at least a few seconds.

- You can then shift back to the social environment. Keep your focus on the conversation, and try to listen mindfully and contribute as well. Try to repeat these tips throughout the meal.

With enough practice, you can better understand when to tune in and shift your attention to your meal and your body. Without letting go of the social interactions and your awareness about the other person at that moment, you can find this understanding as well. A combination of a mindful eating practice and a formal meditation practice can result in a sort of meta-awareness when you stay present and aware of the conversation taking place and your eating experience at the same time.

STRATEGIES FOR EATING MINDFULLY AT RESTAURANTS

Try to make eating out at restaurants a positive experience for your body. It can become very easy for you to overeat when you're at a restaurant or to order the types of food that are not good for your health and well-being. The following tips can help guide you towards a healthier and more mindful ordering and eating experience whether you eat out frequently or just as a special treat:

- If possible, check out the menus ahead of time. Doing so can help you assess your options so you can eliminate the options you don't want and also give you ideas for what may work well for you.
- Consider sharing or avoiding extras such as appetizers, drinks, chips, bread, and desserts. It can be easy to consume them thoughtlessly, and it can leave you feeling unnecessarily uncomfortable and full at the end of the meal. Try to savor the food items you choose to eat mindfully.
- Depending upon your hunger levels and the size of the portion, you can stick to the main dish or even share one.
- You can control how much is served according to

your preference by asking for dressings and sauces on the side.

- If you can't finish a meal because you feel full, take it home so that it doesn't stay on the table and tempt you.
- Practice the techniques of mindful eating and mindful social engagement. You can periodically shift your attention away from your conversation and onto your eating experience. Savor the moments and enjoy with all your senses. Periodically check your levels of hunger and satiety and stop eating when you feel satisfied. You can also practice meta-awareness.

Call to Action:

Take the opportunity to practice some of the above strategies while out and about with friends or co-workers. Take your next social moment to implement one or two things above. How did that feel for you? Would you be able to do that again?

10

MINDFUL EATING MOVING FORWARD

Anything worth working towards in life, including incorporating mindful moments, takes practice. If you have ever learned anything and been on the other side of learning the task or practicing the task, then you know when you get to the other side, it feels great! For example, when you first learned how to ride a bike, it might have felt very challenging. Or, if you remember what it felt like to learn how to tie your shoes or take on a new sport. Similarly, other tasks like meditation or learning a specific move on yoga can take quite a bit of time and practice. However, when you get that move down, it can feel exhilarating. You just accomplished something amazing! The same goes for mindful eating. It can take time. Have patience with yourself! It's not something that may come as fast as riding a bike or learning how to skate. It will take time, and that's okay!

As I have explained in the previous chapters, mindful eating is not a diet. It does not involve radical cleanses, or fads, clearing out your cupboards, or eliminating particular food items. It is certainly not a quick fix. It does not include molding your body into shape; it's not here to instruct you that you should eat particular food items and avoid others, or help you increase your strength. Although it enables you to get physically healthier, it not here just to do one task. Mindful eating simply allows you to be aware of your food choices by letting you savor your food without any personal commentary, anxiety, guilt, shame, or judgment. It helps you to build a better relationship with food.

On any given day, how often do you think about food? For example, you might travel past a fruit stand on your way to the office, or maybe mid-morning, your attention might switch to what you're going to eat for lunch. Perhaps in the evening, you start craving a big, juicy steak. Maybe all you can think about is that piece of cake waiting for you in your fridge. However, it's not right to blame food for any of these thoughts. It is just an object of our cravings and fascination. In itself, it has no power over us. The power only rests in our decisions, our conditioning, feelings, and emotions. We unknowingly trained ourselves to listen to messages portrayed in magazines or social media and voices from the past. We might eat everything on our plates or restrict ourselves because we are obsessed with losing weight because that's what has been drummed into our minds.

Unlike conventional diets, which sometimes add to our stress around eating, and bring lots of pressure, intensity, and false expectations, mindful eating practices create space for you to focus on your mental wellness away from labeling foods and seeing them as good or bad. By embracing mindful eating, you can learn how to find a weight that is actually right for you and not based on the standards of society. It allows you to step away from a culture that tells you that you must be thin to have value or worth. Because of the popular diet culture, some of us also tend to view food as a punishment or reward. Mindful eating changes the way we experience food and allows us to come to a place of freedom away from the bondage that holds us captive to identifying food as a particular thing. It lets us get in touch with our creative sides, our calm, our breath, our awareness.

There can be no room for change without understanding the feelings and thoughts that are involved in our relationship with food. One of the biggest realizations that accompany mindful eating is how much we are affected by our thoughts and feelings. Food is fuel. We require food to live. We can weaken its hold on us and learn not to treat ourselves so harshly once we get a handle on our feelings and thoughts surrounding food. Following mindfulness makes us realize that the way we behave most of the time is mind over matter and understanding that we can get to a place where food is not such a significant source of stress.

Remember that everybody is different. Everyone has a different relationship with food. There is no perfect way to implement mindful eating and no ideal way to eat. Each one of us has our own priorities, preferences, metabolisms, and genetics. Knowing who we are can significantly help us with figuring out what works well for our body and what doesn't work well. Knowing our thoughts and feelings around foods can assist greatly in what we choose. Mindful eating can help bring us to a place of knowing what is right for our bodies and our health.

Practicing mindful eating day to day is all about showing ourselves kindness. It is a kinder approach to eating. It is about instilling mindfulness in our everyday lives and including moments that will make us live more intentionally. It's not necessarily about, although it can be, changing the foods we eat, however, more about changing how we think about the food we eat. By gaining awareness about your food habits, you can explore the reasons behind them in a better way and implement strategies to change them. For example, if you crave control and beat yourself up for even a small diet 'mistake,' you could work on practicing acceptance or self-compassion so that you won't be so hard on yourself when your diet is not perfect. If you fear the mundane and think that eating healthy foods could be very dull, you could buy a cookbook and teach yourself some fun and creative recipes to prepare healthy meals. Or, if you are a pleaser and easily cave into other people's food choices, you could practice assertiveness, maybe by inviting your friend to eat at a healthier restaurant of your choice.

You can practice mindful eating techniques from day to day by choosing foods that will help you feel full. As you already know, it takes almost twenty minutes for your brain to register satiety. Eat slowly and take small bites. Give yourself time to feel the fullness cues so that you can better gauge when you feel full without having to wait for twenty minutes. I challenge you to go through all of the Call to Action moments one more time, week to week, to see once again how this feels.

Call to Action:

Practice all the Call to Action given in the previous chapters for a second time. Do this fully two times through and see how you feel. Bring these mindful moments into your day to day picture.

LEAVE A 1-CLICK REVIEW!

I would be so thankful if you could take just 60 seconds to write a review on Amazon! Even just a few sentences would be amazing!

CONCLUSION

Mindful eating can be defined as a non-judgmental awareness of emotional as well as physical sensations related to eating. It is all about being aware of the way you feel while consuming food. To break it down, even more, mindful eating has four characteristics.

When you're practicing mindful eating, you are:

- Being aware of your emotions, physical hunger, and the cues that alert you when your hunger is satiated.
- Use all of your senses to acknowledge your responses to the food items without any judgment (for example, whether you like the texture, taste, smell, etc. of the food or not)

- Using all your senses to choose the food and experience it. It will be both nourishing to your body and satisfying to you.
- Staying aware of your actions and how it's affecting your body – both good and bad effects.

Eating mindfully is just about maintaining an in-the-moment awareness about the food and drinks you consume, observing instead of judging how it makes you feel, and the signals sent by our body regarding the taste, satisfaction, and fullness. You can then accept and acknowledge the bodily sensations, thoughts, emotions, and feelings you observe. In this book, I have provided you with all the ways you can do so.

Eating mindfully is not about being perfect. It's not about always eating the right foods, or never allowing yourself to eat your favorite foods on-the-go again. More importantly, it's not about establishing strict rules regarding which food items you have to avoid or include in your diet, or how many calories you can consume. Instead, it involves focusing all your senses and being present when you eat, cook, serve, or shop for your food.

You can learn to enjoy both your food and the eating experience. By paying close attention to your feelings when you eat, you learn how different food items affect your mood and energy levels, how the texture and taste of each mouthful feels, and the hunger and fullness signals of your body, etc. You can then begin to find peace in your mind. Practicing mindful eating has several health benefits, including influencing wiser food choices in the future, improving digestion, and feeling full with less food. It can also help you free yourself from unhealthy eating habits.

As already mentioned in the book, eating mindfully can help you to:

- Eat in a more balanced and healthier way.
- Make a better connection with your food, how it's produced, and how it reaches your plate.
- Feel satiated sooner by consuming less food.
- Improve your digestion by eating slower.
- By keeping your focus on how you feel after eating each kind of food, you can make healthier choices regarding what you eat.
- As you learn to slow down and appreciate your snacks and meals more, you can get greater pleasure from the foods you eat.
- Examine and alter your relationship with food, which could help you realize when you're turning to food for reasons other than hunger. It could help

you differentiate between emotional and physical hunger.

- Ease your stress and anxiety by slowing down and taking a break from the day's hustle and bustle.
- Nourishment to the mind, soul, heart, and body.

One of the most significant benefits of mindful eating is that it can help you lose weight by building healthier choices regarding food. Several studies have linked mindful eating with successful weight loss and weight management in women as well as men who were categorized as obese. Another study reported that people who followed mindful eating ate smaller serving sizes of high-calorie foods that supported their weight loss journeys. Also, mindful eating encourages you to deeply connect with your physical need for food and the adverse effects of overeating on your mind and body, unlike typical dieting, which often creates feelings of deprivation. Another essential benefit of mindful eating is that it helps support psychological wellbeing. Our emotional states are affected in different ways by different kinds of foods. So, you can exercise better control over your emotional wellbeing by approaching eating with mindfulness. It also helps to identify emotional and reactive patterns of eating that can result in poor emotional health.

When you first heard of mindful eating, you might have

thought that it's unrealistic to be aware of every bite you eat or every meal you eat. The reality is that you do not have to be aware of every single bite. Thank goodness! You have been provided with a simple solution to help. Just take a few deep breaths before you start eating a snack or a meal and quietly ask yourself whether you are eating because you're hungry or are you eating in response to an emotion. Ask yourself, are you eating because you feel lonely, anxious, or bored. Similarly, is the food you're eating nutritionally healthy or is it emotionally comforting. Finding the answers to these questions through the techniques of mindful eating, as mentioned in the book, will definitely guide you towards better health.

One of the most important things that you should always remember while practicing eating mindfully is that it is not a diet. It does not have any quick fixes. It does not require you to clear out your cupboard and eliminate certain foods. You can think of mindful eating as an exercise – every little bit counts. The more you can slow down and keep your focus solely on the eating process and listening to your body, the greater control you'll have on your eating and nutritional habits and the greater satisfaction you'll get from your food.

Just as I had promised at the beginning of the book, I hope I have been able to provide you with a better understanding of the concepts of mind-body connections and how you can differentiate between what your body needs and what you merely want. I hope I have been able to guide you through all the hurdles that you may face while practicing mindfulness and towards a better and more improved healthy lifestyle.

MINDFUL MOMENTS
CHECKLIST

RESOURCES

Mindful eating. (2011, 2 1). Retrieved from Harvard Health Publishing: https://www.health.harvard.edu/staying-healthy/mindful-eating

Bjorntorp, P. (2001). Do stress reactions cause abdominal obesity and comorbidities? *Obesity Reviews, 2*(2), 73-86.

Carolyn Dunn, M. H. (2018). Mindfulness Approaches and Weight Loss, Weight Maintenance, and Weight Regain. *Current Obesity Reports, 7*(1), 37-49.

Danielle V. Shelov, S. S. (2009). A Pilot Study Measuring the Impact of Yoga on the Trait of Mindfulness. *Behavioral and Cognitive Psychotherapy, 37*(5), 595-598.

Djin Gie Liem, C. G. (2019). The Influence of Taste Liking

on the Consumption of Nutrient Rich and Nutrient Poor Foods. *Frontiers in Nutrition, 6*, 38-45.

Fang Wang, J. K.-K. (2013). The Effects of Qigong on Anxiety, Depression, and Psychological Well-Being: A Systematic Review and Meta-Analysis. *Evidence-Based Complementary and Alternative Medicine*, 1-16.

G. A. O'Reilly, L. C.-M. (2014). Mindfulness-based interventions for obesity-related eating behaviors: a literature review. *Obesity Reviews, 15*(6), 453-461.

Gemma López-Guimerà, H. S.-C. (2014). CLOCK 3111 T/C SNP Interacts with Emotional Eating Behavior for Weight-Loss in a Mediterranean Population. *PLoS ONE, 9*(6), e99152.

Heather M. Niemeier, T. L. (2012). An Acceptance-Based Behavioral Intervention for Weight Loss: A Pilot Study. *Behavior Therapy, 43*(2), 427-435.

Jean L. Kristeller, C. B. (1999). An Exploratory Study of a Meditation-based Intervention for Binge Eating Disorder. *Journal of Health Psychology, 4*(3), 357-363.

Jeanne Dalen, B. W. (2010). Pilot study: Mindful Eating and Living (MEAL): Weight, eating behavior, and psychological outcomes associated with a mindfulness-based intervention for people with obesity. *Complementary Therapies in Medicine, 18*(6), 260-264.

Jennifer Daubenmier, J. K. (2011). Mindfulness Intervention for Stress Eating to Reduce Cortisol and Abdominal Fat among Overweight and Obese Women: An Exploratory Randomized Controlled Study. *Journal of Obesity*, 1-13.

Jennifer Daubenmier, P. J. (2016). Effects of a mindfulness-based weight loss intervention in adults with obesity: A randomized clinical trial. *Obesity, 24*(4), 794-804.

Jetro J. Tuulari, L. T. (2017). Feeding Releases Endogenous Opioids in Humans. *The Journal of Neuroscience, 37*(34), 8284-8291.

Kabat-Zinn, J. (1991). *Full catastrophe living: using the wisdom of your body and mind to face stress, pain, and illness.* New York: Dell Publishing.

Lindsay Maxwell, E. D. (2016). Mindfulness: An Effective Prescription for Depression and Anxiety. *The Journal for Nurse Practitioners, 12*(6), 403-409.

Liye Zou, A. Y. (2018). A Systematic Review and Meta-Analysis of Mindfulness-Based (Baduanjin) Exercise for Alleviating Musculoskeletal Pain and Improving Sleep Quality in People with Chronic Diseases. *International*

Journal of Environmental Research and Public Health, 15(2), 206-45.

Mary P Bennett, J. M. (2003). The Effect of Mirthful Laughter on Stress and Natural Killer Cell Activity. *Alternative therapies in health and medicine*, 38-45.

Michael A. Grodin, L. P. (2008). Treating Survivors of Torture and Refugee Trauma: A Preliminary Case Series Using Qigong and T'ai Chi. *The Journal of Alternative and Complementary Medicine, 14*(7), 801-806.

Monica Beshara, A. D. (2013). Does mindfulness matter? Everyday mindfulness, mindful eating, and self-reported serving size of energy dense foods among a sample of South Australian adults. *Appetite, 67*, 25-29.

Nelson, J. B. (2017). Mindful Eating: The Art of Presence While You Eat. *Diabetes Spectrum, 30*(3), 171-174.

R. S. Crane, J. B.-Z. (2016). What defines mindfulness-based programs? The warp and the weft. *Psychological Medicine, 47*(6), 990-999.

Ray Marks. (2017). Qigong Exercise and Arthritis. *Medicines, 4*(4), 71-45.

Reine C. van der Wal, L. F. (2013). Leaving a Flat Taste in Your Mouth. *Psychological Science, 24*(7), 1277-1284.

Renee B. Cadzow, T. J. (2009). The Association Between Perceived Social Support and Health Among Patients at a Free Urban Clinic. *Journal of the National Medical Association, 101*(3), 243-250.

Richard A. Grucza, T. R. (2007). Prevalence and correlates of binge eating disorder in a community sample. *Comprehensive Psychiatry, 48*(2), 124-131.

Shawn N. Katterman, B. M. (2014). Mindfulness meditation as an intervention for binge eating, emotional eating, and weight loss: A systematic review. *Eating Behaviors, 15*(2), 197-204.

Shawn N. Katterman, B. M. (2014). Mindfulness meditation as an intervention for binge eating, emotional eating, and weight loss: A systematic review. *Eating Behaviors, 15*(2), 197-204.

Shelley E. Taylor, L. C. (2000). Biobehavioral responses to stress in females: Tend-and-befriend, not fight-or-flight. *Psychological Review, 107*(3), 411-429.

Xingjiang Xiong, P. W. (2015). Qigong for Hypertension. *Medicine, 94*(1), e352-45.

Zaimin Li, S. L. (2019). Mind–Body Exercise for Anxiety and Depression in COPD Patients: A Systematic Review and

Meta-Analysis. *International Journal of Environmental Research and Public Health, 17*(1), 22-45.

Printed in Great Britain
by Amazon

86991250R10098